ON ABRAHAM LINCOLN

Lincoln was not a perfect man, nor a perfect president. By modern standards, his condemnation of slavery might be considered tentative.

Chicago Tribune, June 26, 2005

I'm fascinated by Lyndon Johnson; there's a piece of him in me. That kind of hunger—desperate to win, please, succeed, dominate—I don't know any politician who doesn't have some of that reptilian side to him. But that's not the dominant part of me. On the other hand, I don't know that it was the dominant part of Lincoln. The guy was pretty reflective.

Men's Vogue, Fall 2006

I cannot swallow whole the view of Lincoln as the Great Emancipator.

Time Magazine, June 26, 2005

ON AFGHANISTAN

I have always thought that we did the right thing in Afghanistan. My only concern with respect to Afghanistan was that we diverted our attention from Afghanistan in terms of moving into Iraq, and I think would could have done a better job of stabilizing that country than we have in providing assistance to the Afghani people. All of us should be rooting for the Afghani people and making sure that we are providing them the support to make things happen.

Illinois Senate Debate, Illinois Radio Network, October 12, 2004

ON AFRICA

Africans are going to have to be responsible for their own salvation. We have to be partners with them in that process. The African-American community here has to be attentive to their issues. On the flip side, African leaders have to create a rule of law that is not corrupt, that is transparent.

Essence, October 2006

Black Americans have always had an ambiguous relationship with Africa. Nowadays, we wear *kente* cloth, celebrate Kwanza and put up posters of Nelson Mandela on our walls. And when we travel to Africa and discover it's not all sweetness and light, we can end up deeply disappointed.

Crisis, October 1995

ON THE AFRICAN-AMERICAN COMMUNITY

I don't think the Democratic Party takes the African-American voters for granted. I want Republicans to compete for the African-American vote. They're not getting the African-American vote not because African-Americans aren't open-minded, but because Democrats have consistently championed those issues—civil rights, voting rights, concern for working families—that are of greatest concern to African-American voters.

Meet the Press, July 25, 2004

In the African-American community in particular, I think sometimes we have a tendency for our leadership to be very protective of their turf and not invite young people in until it's way too late. The earlier we're grooming young people and giving them leadership opportunities, and pushing them up front, the better.

Black Collegian, October 2006

I firmly believe the overwhelming majority of African-Americans are just as hardworking, just as intent to go about their business. What is true, though, is sometimes we get into the mode of it's easier to blame white folks for things than us taking the responsibility.

Who's Afraid of a Large Black Man? Charles Barkley, page 35

We have a certain script in our politics, and one of the scripts for black politicians is that for them to be authentically black they have to somehow offend white people. And then if he puts a multiracial coalition together, he must somehow be compromising the efforts of the African-American community. To use a street term, we flipped the script.

Chicago Tribune, June 26, 2005

I think that it is the best of times and the worst of times for the African-American community. And one of the things that I want to make certain is that the voices of young men standing on a street corner without hope and vision for the future. Voices are heard in the U.S. Senate, that we feel a certain sense of urgency about a generation that we're losing.

All Things Considered, July 27, 2004

Any black person in America who's successful has to be able to speak several different forms of the same language. You take on different personas as you need to, when you have to. There's nothing wrong with it. You're going to speak differently on the golf course with your golf buddies than you are with your buddies around the kitchen table.

Who's Afraid of a Large Black Man? Charles Barkley, page 25

10

I know if I'm in an all-black audience that there's going to be a certain rhythm coming back at me from the audience. They're not just going to be sitting there. That creates a different rhythm in your speaking.

Chicago Tribune, June 26, 2005

ON AIDS

We are all sick because of AIDS—and we are all tested by this crisis. Neither philanthropist nor scientist; neither government nor church, can solve this problem on their own—AIDS must be an all-hands-on-deck effort.

World AIDS Day Speech, December 1, 2006

I don't think we can deny that there is a moral and spiritual component to prevention. Again and again I heard stories of men and women contracting HIV because sex was no longer part of a sacred covenant, but a mechanical physical act. Having said that, I also believe that we cannot ignore that abstinence and fidelity may too often be the ideal and not the reality. If condoms and potentially microbicides can prevent millions of deaths, they should be made more widely available.

Orange County Register, December 1, 2006

I think it's important that we target HIV/AIDS resources in the communities where we're seeing the highest growth rates. That means education and prevention, particularly with young people. It means that we have to look at drastic measures like needle exchange in order to insure that drug users are not transmitting the disease to each other. And we've got to expand on treatment programs. And all of that is going to cost some money and some time. But the more we invest in that ounce of prevention the better off we're going to be.

Politico.com, February 11, 2008

ON THE AMERICAN CHARACTER

Never forget that we have it within our power to shape history in this country. It is not in our character to sit idly by as victims of fate or circumstance, for we are a people of action and innovation, forever pushing the boundaries of what's possible.

"Cutting Costs and Covering America: A Twenty-first Century Health Care System," University of Iowa, May 29, 2007

ON THE AMERICAN DREAM

Stay amazed, and remain in wonder at this unlikely place we call America. I think it's easy for some people to look at all the challenges we face; to look at poverty and war and racism and inequality and hatred and helplessness, and to get down on this country as a result. To think that there's something wrong with us and that there is little hope to make things better. If you ever feel like that yourselves, I ask you to remember all the amazing and unlikely things that have happened in this country. This is America. A place where millions of restless adventurers from all over the world, still weary of their lot in life—still hoping for something better—have longed to travel great distances and take great risks for a chance to arrive on our shores.

University of Massachusetts at Boston Commencement Address,
June 2, 2006

This country remains the greatest on Earth, not because of the size of our military or the size of our economy, but because every child can actually achieve as much as they can dream.

Meet the Press, July 25, 2004

In big cities and small towns; among men and women; young and old; black, white, and brown—Americans share a faith in simple dreams. A job with wages that can support a family. Health care that we can count on and afford. A retirement that is dignified and secure. Education and opportunity for our kids. Common hopes. American dreams.

"Remarks of Senator Barack Obama: Reclaiming the American Dream." Bettendorf, Iowa, November 7, 2007

Tonight we proved once more that the true strength of our nation comes not from the might of our arms or the scale of our wealth, but from the enduring power of our ideals: democracy, liberty, opportunity, and unyielding hope.

Presidential acceptance speech, Grant Park, Chicago, Illinois, November 4, 2008

ON BEING A CHRISTIAN

You need to come to church in the first place precisely because you are first of this world, not apart from it. You need to embrace Christ precisely because you have sins to wash away—because you are human and need an ally in this difficult journey.

Call to Renewal Keynote Address, June 28, 2006

There are still passages that I read in the Bible where I say, Well, this doesn't make any sense.

New Yorker, October 30, 2006

I am a Christian, and I am a devout Christian. I believe in the redemptive death and resurrection of Jesus Christ. I believe that that faith gives me a path to be cleansed of sin and have eternal life.

Christianity Today, January 2008

16

We should never forget that God granted us the power to reason so that we would do His work here on Earth.

World AIDS Day Speech, December 1, 2006

My faith is one that admits some doubt.

ABC's *This Week with George Stephanopoulos*, August 15, 2004

It's an ongoing process for all of us in making sure that we are living out our faith every day. It's something that I try to pray on at the beginning of every day and at the end of every day, whether I'm living my life in a way that's consistent with my faith. The prayer that I tell myself every night is a fairly simple one: I ask in the name of Jesus Christ that my sins are forgiven, that my family is protected, and that I am an instrument of God's will. I'm constantly trying to align myself to what I think He calls on me to do.

Beliefnet.com, January 2008

ON BIPARTISANSHIP

Senator Tom Coburn of Oklahoma is the best kind of conservative because he's a sincere conservative. He's not just trying to score political points. We all have an interest in making sure our money is well spent.

Knight Ridder Tribune, October 20, 2006

I'm not somebody comfortable with liberal-conservative labels. What the American people are looking for are commonsense solutions.

Meet the Press, July 25, 2004

To me, the issue is not are you centrist or are you liberal? The issue to me is, Is what you're proposing going to work? Can you build a working coalition to make the lives of people better? And if it can work, you should support it whether it's centrist, conservative, or liberal.

New York Magazine, October 2, 2006

ON BLUE STATES AND RED STATES

With the red-state phenomenon where Democrats just say, well, we can't campaign in those areas because they're going to vote Republican, I think that's a mistake.

Face the Nation, March 12, 2006

There is a faction on the right that is very absolutist and there's a portion of the left that is the same way, demonizing the other side. And then there are eighty percent of people in the middle.

Rolling Stone, December 30, 2004

These either/or formulations are wearisome. They're not useful. The reality outstrips the mental categories we're operating in.

New York Magazine, October 2, 2006

ON BOOKS THAT HAVE INSPIRED HIM

I remember reading [Studs Terkel's] *Working* when it first came out and just finding that very powerful. What stuck was to reveal the sacredness of ordinary people's lives. That everybody has a story. And I think Studs is terrific at drawing out that shimmering quality of people's everyday struggles.

Chicago Tribune, October 26, 2006

Right around my first year of college, I read *Song of Solomon*, by Toni Morrison, it just moved me tremendously. The power of language and how it can peel back truths, bring things to the surface.

Chicago Tribune, October 26, 2006

ON CAMPAIGN FINANCE REFORM

Real reform means making sure that members of Congress and the administration tell us when they're negotiating for jobs with industries they're responsible for regulating. That way we don't have people writing a drug bill during the day and meeting with pharmaceutical companies about their future salary at night.

Speech to the Chicago Council on Foreign Relations, November 22, 2005

The underlying issue of how extensively money influences politics is the original sin of everyone who's ever run for office—myself included. In order to get elected, we need to raise vast sums of money by meeting and dealing with people who are disproportionately wealthy.

Speech at the Lobbying Reform Summit, January 26, 2006

The biggest advantage that big money has in Washington is a host of full-time lobbyists who can track that one bill that, for their client, means a billion-dollar tax break, but that nobody else even knows is there.

New Yorker, October 30, 2006

The whole issue of money in politics is one that I'm constantly struggling with, because my preference would be that we've got public financing of campaigns and nobody has to raise money whatsoever.

All Things Considered, October 19, 2006

Even if we pass a good bill and rid Washington of the Jack Abramoffs of the world, it's going to take much more than gift bans and lobbying reform to restore the public's faith in a government. It will take not simply a change in laws, but a change in attitudes. To earn back that trust—to show people that we're working for them and looking out for their interests—we have to start acting like it.

Speech to the Chicago Council on Foreign Relations, November 22, 2005

ON HIS CHILDHOOD

I was such a terror that my teachers didn't know what to do with me.

Harper's, November 2006

Growing up, I absorbed a lot of negative stereotypes about how I should behave as a black teenager and fell into some of the same traps that a lot of black male youth do. It wasn't preordained that I would go to Columbia or to Harvard. I didn't have a father in the house, which meant that I didn't have a lot of role models in terms of how I should operate.

Chicago Tribune, June 26, 2005

When I was a kid I inhaled. That was the point.

Economist, October 28, 2006

My mother taught me not to reject a compliment when it's offered.

Letter to *The Black Commentator*, June 19, 2003

ON HIS CHILDREN

My little girls can break my heart. They can make me cry just looking at them eating their string beans.

Houston Chronicle, October 29, 2006

One of the wrestling matches I'm always having with my staff is getting my kids' events onto the schedule. I have to make sure they understand that's a priority.

Live Your Best Life, Oprah Winfrey, page 294

When I sit down with my six-year-old and my three-year-old at night and I'm reading a book to them and then I tuck them in to go to sleep, that's a little piece of heaven that I hang onto.

American Libraries, August 2005

ON CHINA

The U.S. should be firm on issues that divide us [from the Beijing government]—like Taiwan—while flexible on issues that could unite us. We should insist on labor standards and human rights, the opening of Chinese markets fully to American goods, and the fulfillment of legal contracts with American businesses, but without triggering a trade war, as prolonged instability in the Chinese economy could have global economic consequences.

"Renewal of American Leadership" press release, July 12, 2004

China is rising, and it's not going away. They're neither our enemy nor our friend.

Democratic primary presidential debate, April 26, 2007

I intend to forge a more effective regional framework in Asia that will promote stability [and] prosperity and help us confront common transnational threats such as tracking down terrorists and responding to global health problems like avian flu.

Remarks to the Chicago Council on Global Affairs, April 23, 2007

ON HIS CIGARETTE HABIT

I smoked for a long time and quit, and occasionally I lapse back into it. It's an ongoing struggle.

Knight Ridder Tribune, October 20, 2006

I'm a reformed smoker; I think that surprises people. I quit, but then during the campaign when you're in a car driving through cornfields, occasionally I bum a cigarette or two. But I did all my drinking in high school and college. I was a wild man. I did drugs and drank and partied. But I got all my ya-yas out.

Rolling Stone, December 30, 2004

Nicorette has worked. You're supposed to phase out the stuff, but I haven't completely. I'm still chewing.

Politico.com, February 11, 2008

ON THE CLINTONS

I think that there's a difference, obviously, between the Bushes and the Clintons. But I do think that Washington is comfortable with itself. And I think the Clintons are part of that status quo that has to change itself.

60 Minutes, February 7, 2008

ON CONGRESS

This has been a very unproductive Congress since I've arrived there. Hopefully, though, there's no correlation between my arrival and the lack of productivity. I've been in the minority and I haven't been able to move a lot of legislation forward because frankly those who have been in charge of the Senate, the Republican majority, haven't been interested in the work that I've been doing.

Larry King Live, October 19, 2006

ON HIS CRITICS

It's not that I'm being cautious. It's that I disagree with them.

Time, February 20, 2006

ON THE CURRENT STATE OF POLITICS

It's 24-hour, slash-and-burn, negative-ad, bickering, small-minded politics that doesn't move us forward.

Milwaukee Journal Sentinel, December 11, 2006

Politics in Washington has become the intellectual equivalent of WWF Wrestling: smacking each other, throwing chairs, but nothing really gets done.

Houston Chronicle, October 29, 2006

We can play Reverend Wright's sermons on every channel, every day and talk about them from now until the election, and make the only question in this campaign whether or not the American people think that I somehow believe or sympathize with his most offensive words. We can pounce on some gaffe by a Hillary supporter as evidence that she's playing the race card, or we can speculate on whether white men will all flock to John McCain in the general election regardless of his policies. We can do that. But if we do, I can tell you that in the next election, we'll be talking about some other distraction. And then another one. And then another one. And nothing will change.

"A More Perfect Union" Philadelphia, Pennsylvania, March 18, 2008

ON DARFUR

We should be engaged in Darfur. We have a self-interest and a stake in preventing hundreds of thousands of people from being slaughtered.

New Yorker, January 15, 2007

The United States should raise the needed funds to ensure that the civilians in Sudan receive life-saving humanitarian assistance. We should lead in contributing the lion's share of these funds so that we can convince others to give their fair share as well. Next, the United States should support the immediate deployment of an effective international force to disarm militias, protect civilians, and facilitate delivery of humanitarian assistance in Darfur.

Speech, October 7, 2004

We have a strong national security interest. If you start seeing more and more failed states, more and more displaced persons, more and more refugees, all of that becomes a breeding ground for terrorist activity, it becomes a breeding ground for disease, and it creates refugees that put pressure on our own borders. In an interconnected world we can't insulate ourselves from these tragedies. We're going to have to develop some strategy as the world's remaining super-power to address these issues, and Darfur is an important test case. We've already failed one test in Rwanda, we shouldn't fail another.

"Darfur: Current Policy Not Enough" podcast, February 15, 2006

ON HIS DECISION TO RUN FOR PRESIDENT

This is a profoundly personal decision that I'm going through. I'm looking at the external factors: money, organization, calendar, all those things. But the most important thing I'm looking at is, Do I have something unique to bring to a presidential race that would justify putting my family through what I think everybody understands is a grueling process?

Chicago Tribune, November 20, 2006

I think I was first asked [if I was going to run for president] the day after I'd been elected to the Senate. It was an eight-in-the-morning press conference, I'd just come out of the election, and I remember laughing at the question because presumably it would make sense for me to be sworn into my new office before I started thinking about the next one.

All Things Considered, October 19, 2006

The decision to run for president is a very serious one. And it's a very humbling decision. I have to feel that I have something unique to offer the country that no other person can provide right now.

Ebony, February 2007

The one thing I'm clear about in terms of the presidency is that it can't be something you pursue on the basis of vanity and ambition. There's a certain soberness and seriousness required.

Meet the Press, October 22, 2006

What's happened is that we create this parlor game where, you know, there's constant speculation and is this person running, is this person not running. And then candidates who do decide to run end up stretching out their announcement over the course of the year and make four different announcements

All Things Considered, October 19, 2006

My general attitude is that if I'm doing a good job in what I'm doing now, I can have the opportunity to seek higher office. If I'm not doing a good job and paying too much attention to what could happen down the road, that option won't be open to me.

Essence, October 2006

Running for the presidency is a profound decision—a decision no one should make on the basis of media hype or personal ambition alone—and so before I committed myself and my family to this race, I wanted to be sure that this was right for us, and more importantly, right for the country.

Barackobama.com, January 16, 2007

I certainly didn't expect to find myself in this position a year ago. But as I've spoken to many of you in my travels, I've been struck by how hungry we all are for a different kind of politics.

USA Today, January 17, 2007

I was never the likeliest candidate for this office.

> Presidential acceptance speech, Grant Park, Chicago, Illinois,
> November 4, 2008

ON DEMOCRACY

There's always going to be some conflict in democracy. It's a big country. It's a complicated country. Democracy is messy. And a lot of that is healthy.

> *Charlie Rose Show*, October 19, 2006

ON THE DEMOCRATIC PARTY

The belief in each other—that's what made me a Democrat.

San Francisco Chronicle, October 28, 2006

The party has not updated its vision and its message. We haven't painted a picture of where we want to take the country.

Essence, October 2006

This is our time and I'm grateful to be a part of that.

Democratic fundraiser in Manchester, New Hampshire,
December 12, 2006

The Democratic Party has always stood for giving everyone an equal chance, despite the circumstances of their birth. My story is emblematic of that. I want to affirm those values.

National Review, July 27, 2004

The Democratic Party has not told a good story. What we have are a series of policy prescriptions to solve particular issues. We have our environmental position and our labor position and our health-care position, but we don't have a narrative. And the Republicans do.

Rolling Stone, December 30, 2004

I think there's a false choice being presented in the Democratic Party right now, between those who argue that our job is to oppose everything George Bush does and cling to the old-time religion, or the faction where you just split the difference and not notice that over a number of years the goalposts are drifting further and further to the right. What I think we have to do is transcend those categories.

Time, February 13, 2006

The Democratic Party is a big tent, which means that there are positions I may not agree with.

Politico.com, February 11, 2008

There are times I think we're not ambitious enough. Back in 2004, one of the candidates had made a proposal about universal health care, and a commentator said, "We can't propose this kind of big-government costly program, because it'll send a signal we're tax-and-spend liberals." But that's not a good reason to not do something. You don't give up on the goal of universal health care because you don't want to be tagged as a liberal.

New York Magazine, October 2, 2006

If the Democrats can't inspire, if they can't tap into some sense of meaning that goes beyond just dollars and cents, then it's going to be very hard for them to argue against the sort of selfishness and self-interested policies that have come to dominate our politics.

All Things Considered, March 10, 2005

If the Democrats are only issuing white papers and policy positions and not talking to people about their central experiences, then I think there are going to be problems.

ABC This Week, November 7, 2004

We've got a story to tell that isn't just against something but is for something. We know that we're the party of opportunity.

Annual Take Back America Conference, June 14, 2006

We as Democrats have not been very interested in poverty or issues relating to the inner city as much as we should have. Think about the last presidential campaign: It's pretty hard to focus a moment on which there was any attention given.

Chicago Tribune, September 11, 2005

ON DIVERSITY

I believe in vigorous enforcement of our nondiscrimination laws. But I also believe that a transformation of conscience and a genuine commitment to diversity on the part of the nation's CEOs could bring about quicker results than a battalion of lawyers. They have more lawyers than us anyway.

Call to Renewal Keynote Address, June 28, 2006

Religious people are far more tolerant than I think the popular culture gives them credit for. Conversely, secularists are far more interested in morality and ethics than the right wing would portray them.

Charlie Rose Show, October 19, 2006

I'm well situated to help the country understand how we can both celebrate our diversity in all its complexity and still affirm our common bonds. Maybe I can help with that because I've got so many different pieces in me.

Live Your Best Life, Oprah Winfrey, page 293

ON EDUCATION

I think that community colleges are going to play an increasingly critical role, because one thing we know for certain about the changing
economy is that nobody is going to have a permanent job.

Community College Week, March 28, 2005

No longer can we assume that a high-school education in Boston is
enough to compete for a job that could easily go to a college-educated
student in Bangalore or Beijing.

University of Massachusetts at Boston Commencement Address,
June 2, 2006

We have an obligation and a responsibility to be investing in our students and our schools. We must make sure that people who have the
grades, the desire and the will, but not the money, can still get the
best education possible.

Black Issues in Higher Education, October 7, 2004

40

It's really important that we revamp our college loan programs to free up more money for students. The direct loan program works extremely well, and there doesn't appear to be a need for these student loan programs to be managed through banks and other private lenders. If we were able to consolidate programs under the Direct Loan program, we would save $4.5 billion, which could be funneled back into providing more Pell grants and providing a higher level of grants per student.

Black Issues in Higher Education, October 7, 2004

No Child Left Behind did not speak to what I think is a critical issue in education, that is how do we encourage our best and brightest to continue teaching, and how do we substantially upgrade the pay and performance of the teaching profession?

Speech at the Aspen Institute, July 2, 2005

We know that in a global economy that's more connective and more competitive that we're the party that will guarantee every American an affordable, world-class, life-long, top-notch education, from early childhood to high school—from college to on-the-job training. We know that that's what we're about.

Annual 2006 Take Back America Conference, June 14, 2006

I try to avoid an either/or approach to solving the problems of this country. There are questions of individual responsibility and questions of societal responsibility to be dealt with. The best example is an education. I'm going to insist that we've got decent funding, enough teachers, and computers in the classroom, but unless you turn off the television set and get over a certain anti-intellectualism that I think pervades some low-income communities, our children are not going to achieve.

Meet the Press, July 25, 2004

Our public education system is the key to opportunity for millions of children and families. It needs to be the best in the world. Of particular concern is the growing achievement gap between middle- and low-income students, which has continued to expand despite some overall national achievement gains.

ObamaForIllinois.com, May 2, 2004

ON ENERGY POLICY

As president, I will tap our natural gas reserves, invest in clean coal technology, and find ways to safely harness nuclear power. I'll help our auto companies re-tool, so that the fuel-efficient cars of the future are built right here in America. I'll make it easier for the American people to afford these new cars. And I'll invest $150 billion over the next decade in affordable, renewable sources of energy.

Acceptance speech, Democratic National Convention, August 28, 2008

Here's the deal we can make with the auto companies. It's a piece of legislation I introduced called Health Care for Hybrids, and it would allow the federal government to pick up part of the tab for the auto companies' retiree health care costs. In exchange, the auto companies would then use some of that savings to build and invest in more fuel-efficient cars.

Speech at the Governor's Ethanol Coalition, February 28, 2006

Our persistent dependence on oil is a danger our government has known about for years. And despite constant warnings by researchers and scientists, major corporations and our own government officials, it's a danger they have failed to prepare for, listen to, or seriously try to guard against. It's a danger we can no longer afford to ignore.

"Securing Our Energy Future" speech, September 15, 2005

I would not make huge investments or try to take technologies to scale that worsen the climate-change situation. But it may be appropriate for the federal government to make small investments in pilot projects to see if we can make dirty fuels cleaner.

Outside.com, September 2007

I want to move aggressively on an energy bill because I think that's another area where we have a potential convergence between national security hawks, environmental greens, [and] people who are concerned with their pocketbooks and what's happening at the gas pumps. I think we can really bring the country together around an aggressive energy plan that will involve increasing fuel efficiency standards, ratcheting down greenhouse gas emissions, and setting up an auction for those emissions that generate monies we can use to create a very aggressive exploration for alternative fuels.

Reader's Digest, September 2007

Saying that America is addicted to oil without following a real plan for energy independence is like admitting alcoholism and then skipping the 12-step program.

Chicago Tribune, April 3, 2006

[We should] free America from its dependence on foreign oil. We must take concrete steps to move us toward energy independence including requiring that 20 percent of the nation's power supply portfolio come from renewable sources like wind, solar, biomass, and geothermal energy by 2020, and that a percentage of our nation's fuel supply is provided by renewable fuels such as ethanol and biodiesel.

"Renewal of American Leadership" press release, July 12, 2004

I voted for the last energy bill because it took some baby steps in the right direction. It invests in the renewable, homegrown biofuels that could turn out to be some of the most promising alternatives to oil. The solutions are too timid, the reforms too small. A bill that reduces our dependency on foreign oil by just 3 percent when our demand is about to jump 40 percent is not a serious energy policy. We need to do more.

"Securing Our Energy Future" speech, September 15, 2005

We can't continue to settle for piecemeal, bite-sized solutions to our energy crisis. We need a national commitment to energy security, and to emphasize that commitment, we should install a Director of Energy Security to oversee all of our efforts. Like the Chairman of the Joint Chiefs and the National Intelligence Director, this person would be an advisor to the National Security Council and have the full authority to coordinate America's energy policy across all levels of government.

Speech at the Governor's Ethanol Coalition, February 28, 2006

We could save as much, in terms of our fuel, if we increased our fuel efficiency standards, as much as we would from getting Alaska drilling going immediately. And that's been the Bush strategy: increasing production for oil and gas companies, subsidizing them to the tune of 20 billion dollars, as opposed to thinking about how not only we can develop alternative fuels, but also how can we conserve energy and increase efficiencies available right now but have not been invested in.

Illinois Senate Debate, October 26, 2004

With nuclear power, we have to see if there are ways for us to store the radioactive material in a safe, environmentally sound way—and if we can do that and deal with some of the safety and security issues, it's something that we should look at. We should experiment with all sorts of potential energy sources—don't prejudge what works and what doesn't, but insist that we have very strict standards in terms of where we want to end up, and enforce those standards vigorously.

Outside.com, September 2007

Let's fight to wean ourselves off Middle East oil, through an energy policy that doesn't simply serve the interests of Exxon and Mobil.

Speech at anti-Iraq War rally in Chicago, October 26, 2002

The only thing as predictable as rising gas prices are the short-term political solutions that usually come along with them. Every year you had the same headlines, Pain at the Pump, and then Americans start emptying their wallets to fill up their tanks and politicians go through the standard responses: tax rebates and tax holidays, investigating price-gouging bio-oil companies.

"A Real Solution for High Gas Prices" podcast, May 11, 2006

ON THE ECONOMY

I'd invest in clean energy, to lower demand and lower gas prices and create millions of jobs in clean and renewable energies like wind and solar and biodiesel. I think that would make a huge improvement long-term.

> In response to the question of what would he do if he could do only one thing to improve the economy, *Scranton Times-Tribune*, April 21, 2008

Senator McCain recently admitted his energy proposal for the gas-tax holiday will have mainly "psychological benefits." Now I want all of you to know that America already has one Dr. Phil, we don't need another. When it comes to the economy, we need somebody who can actually solve the economy.

> *Washington Post*, July 7, 2008

Our economy is in shambles.

> *msnbc.com*, April 19, 2008

ON EQUAL RIGHTS

We must be careful to keep our eyes on the prize—equal rights for every American. We must continue to fight for the Employment Non-Discrimination Act. We must vigorously expand hate-crime legislation and be vigilant about how these laws are enforced. We must continue to expand adoption rights to make them consistent and seamless throughout all 50 states, and we must repeal the "Don't Ask, Don't Tell" military policy.

Windy City Times, February 11, 2004

ON EXERCISE

I've held up pretty good [during the primary], but I've been religious about getting my exercise, so I've been working out every morning. We play a little basketball. We realized that we had played basketball before Iowa and before South Carolina, but not before New Hampshire and Nevada. And so now, we've made a clear rule that on Election Day, I have to play basketball.

60 Minutes, February 7, 2008

ON FOREIGN POLICY

American leadership has been a mighty force for human progress. The steady march of democracy and free enterprise across the globe speaks to the steadfastness of our leadership and the power of our ideals. Today we face new and frightful challenges, especially the threat of terror. Never has it been more important for America to lead wisely, to shrewdly project power and wield influence on behalf of liberty and security. Unfortunately, I fear our once great influence is waning, a victim of misguided policies and impetuous actions. Never has the U.S. possessed so much power, and never has the U.S. had so little influence to lead.

Speech to the Chicago Council on Foreign Relations, July 12, 2004

It is absolutely vital that we maintain a strong and active foreign policy, relentless in pursuing our enemies and hopeful in promoting our values around the world.

St. Louis Post-Dispatch, November 20, 2006

I'm proud of the fact that I stood up early and unequivocally in opposition to Bush's foreign policy. That opposition hasn't changed.

Letter to *The Black Commentator*, June 19, 2003

The world is watching what we do today in America. They will know what we do here today, and they will treat all of us accordingly in the future—our soldiers, our diplomats, our journalists, anybody who travels beyond these borders. I hope we remember this as we go forward.

Floor Statement on the Habeas Corpus Amendment,
September 27, 2006

In every region of the globe, our foreign policy should promote traditional American ideals: democracy and human rights; free and fair trade and cultural exchanges; and development of institutions that ensure broad middle classes within market economies. It is our commonality of interests in the world that can ultimately restore our influence and win back the hearts and minds necessary to defeat terrorism and project American values around the globe. Human aspirations are universal—for dignity, for freedom, for the opportunity to improve the lives of our families.

Speech to the Chicago Council on Foreign Relations, July 12, 2004

I think [Americans] instinctively understand that we cannot simply impose our will militarily on the entire globe.

Houston Chronicle, October 29, 2006

People say, surely we can create a foreign policy and a national-security strategy that combines the might of our military with diplomacy. We've done it before. Why can't we do it again?

Seattle Times, October 27, 2006

We still have the chance to correct recent missteps that have put our principles and legacy in question. Indeed, it is imperative to our nation's standing and security to do so. It will take a change of attitude and direction in our national leadership to restore the values and judgment that made and kept our nation the world's beacon of hope and freedom.

Speech to the Chicago Council on Foreign Relations, July 12, 2004

ON FREE TRADE

[My constituents] wear Nike shoes and buy Pioneer stereos. They don't want the borders closed. They just don't want their communities destroyed.

New Yorker, May 31, 2004

My problem with our trade agreements right now is not that I feel we can't compete in the global economy. I think we've got the best workers on earth. I think the problem is that we're not very good bargainers. Our trade mentality dates back to the sixties and early seventies when we were so dominant in the world economy that basically if people sent their goods into this country without reciprocity, it wasn't really going to have a dent on our economy.

CNBC Closing Bell, March 27, 2008

ON THE FUTURE

It's not that ordinary people have forgotten how to dream. It's just that their leaders have forgotten how.

Philadelphia Inquirer, December 11, 2006

It's your turn to keep this daringly radical but unfailingly simple notion of America alive—that no matter where you're born or how much your parents have; no matter what you look like or what you believe in, you can still rise to become whatever you want; still go on to achieve great things; still pursue the happiness you hope for.

University of Massachusetts at Boston Commencement Address,
June 2, 2006

At their core Americans are a decent people. And there is a sense of hope that people can change this country together.

Times of London, December 11, 2006

The true test of the American ideal is whether we're able to recognize our failings and then rise together to meet the challenges of our time. Whether we allow ourselves to be shaped by events and history, or whether we act to shape them.

Knox College Commencement Address, June 4, 2005

ON GAY MARRIAGE

The heightened focus on marriage is a distraction from other, attainable measures to prevent discrimination of gays and lesbians.

The Audacity of Hope, pages 222-3

58

I am somebody who has not embraced gay marriage. I've said that it's not something that I think the society is necessarily ready for. And it strikes me that in a lot of ways for a lot of people, it may intrude in how they understand marriage. But I also think that we should create civil unions for gays and lesbians that allow them to have the same basic rights as all people.

Larry King Live, October 19, 2006

I don't think marriage is a civil right, but I think that not being discriminated against is a civil right.

Illinois Senate Debate, October 26, 2004

I opposed the Defense of Marriage Act in 1996. It should be repealed and I will vote for its repeal on the Senate floor. I will also oppose any proposal to amend the U.S. Constitution to ban gays and lesbians from marrying. I know how important the issue of equal rights is to the LGBT community. I share your sense of urgency.

Windy City Times, February 11, 2004

I opposed the Defense of Marriage Act in 1996. It should be repealed and I will vote for its repeal on the Senate floor. I will also oppose any proposal to amend the U.S. Constitution to ban gays and lesbians from marrying. I know how important the issue of equal rights is to the LGBT community. I share your sense of urgency.

Windy City Times, February 11, 2004

ON GAYS IN THE MILITARY

I reasonably can see "Don't Ask, Don't Tell" eliminated. I think that I can help usher through an Employment Non-Discrimination Act and sign it into law. I think there's increasing recognition within the Armed Forces that this is a counterproductive strategy. We're spending large sums of money to kick highly qualified gays or lesbians out of our military, some of whom possess specialties like Arab-language capabilities that we desperately need. That doesn't make us more safe.

Advocate.com, April 10, 2008

ON GENERATIONAL CONFLICT

A lot of the political arguments that we see now are continuations of arguments that took place in the '60s. What I'm seeing out in the country is, particularly in younger generations, wanting to get beyond some of those arguments and saying to themselves, look, the very personal, very vitriolic, deep-seated animosities that were created in that era are over.

Charlie Rose Show, October 19, 2006

When you watch Clinton vs. Gingrich, or Gore vs. Bush, or Kerry vs. Bush, you feel like these are fights that were taking place back in dorm rooms in the '60s.

Sunday Times Magazine, November 5, 2006

I think that older folks hang on too long and stay in the way. I think that if a young person feels they can do a better job than somebody in the next generation, sometimes it's necessary to go ahead and run, and keep in mind that usually folks don't give up power easily. It has to be wrested from them.

Black Collegian, October 2006

ON GLOBAL WARMING

Maybe there are a couple of holdouts in the White House that don't believe in climate change. But there are 10,000 scientists who believe that maybe we should do something about it.

San Francisco Chronicle, October 28, 2006

What we can be scientifically certain of is that our continued use of fossil fuels is pushing us to a point of no return. And unless we free ourselves from a dependence on these fossil fuels and chart a new course on energy in this country, we are condemning future generations to global catastrophe.

Chicago Tribune, April 6, 2006

ON GLOBALIZATION

As the world continues to change and we become more connected to each other, globalization will bring both benefits and disruptions to our lives. But either way, it's here, and it's not going away. We can try to build walls around us, and we can look inward, and we can respond by being frightened and angry about those disruptions. But that's not what we're about.

University of Massachusetts at Boston Commencement Address,
June 2, 2006

ON GUN CONTROL

I believe in keeping guns out of our inner cities, and that our leaders must say so in the face of the gun manufacturer's lobby. But I also believe that when a gangbanger shoots indiscriminately into a crowd because he feels someone disrespected him, we have a problem of morality. Not only do we need to punish that man for his crime, but we need to acknowledge that there's a hole in his heart, one that government programs alone may not be able to repair.

The Audacity of Hope, page 215

We have two conflicting traditions in this country. I think it's important for us to recognize that we've got a tradition of gun ownership, and a lot of law-abiding citizens use it for hunting, for sportsmanship, and to protect their families. We also have a violence on the streets that is the result of illegal handgun usage. And so I think there is nothing wrong with a community saying we are going to take those illegal handguns off the streets. The problem is that the NRA says any regulation whatsoever is the camel's nose under the tent. And I don't think that's where the American people are at. We can have reasonable, thoughtful gun control measure that still respects the Second Amendment and people's traditions.

Politico.com, February 11, 2008

ON HEALTH CARE

As progressives, we believe in affordable health care for all Americans, and we're going to make sure that Americans don't have to choose between a health care plan that bankrupts the government and one that bankrupts families. The party won't just throw a few tax breaks at families who can't afford their insurance, but will modernize our health care system and give every family a chance to buy insurance at a price they can afford.

Annual Take Back America Conference, June 14, 2006

The prescription drug bill that was passed by Bush was a fundamentally flawed piece of legislation. We have a bill that's bad for taxpayers and bad for senior citizens. Taxpayers are hit with a half-a-trillion-dollar tab that was originally estimated at three hundred billion. And seniors have a big donut hole in the middle of their benefits. What I would do is say that senior citizens, through the Medicare program, can go and negotiate the best possible price as a consequence of being bulk purchasers.

Illinois Senate Debate, Illinois Radio Network, October 12, 2004

Now is the time to finally keep the promise of affordable, accessible health care for every single American. If you have health care, my plan will lower your premiums. If you don't, you'll be able to get the same kind of coverage that members of Congress give themselves.

Acceptance speech, Democratic National Convention,
August 28, 2008

We've got to make sure that we are bringing people into coverage so that they're not going to the emergency room. Short term, that will cost us some money. Long term, the more we emphasize prevention, the less likely we are to pay huge bills down the road. That's the only way we're going to get control of health care inflation.

CNBC Closing Bell, March 27, 2008

We are not a country that rewards hard work and perseverance with bankruptcies and foreclosures. We are not a country that allows major challenges to go unsolved and unaddressed while our people suffer needlessly. In the richest nation on earth, it is simply not right that the skyrocketing profits of the drug insurance industries are paid for by the skyrocketing premiums that come from the pockets of the American people. This is not who we are.

"Cutting Costs and Covering America: a Twenty-first Century Health Care System. University of Iowa, May 29, 2007

The problem is, there's currently no financial incentive for health care providers to offer services that will encourage patients to eat right or exercise or go for annual check-ups and screenings that can help detect diseases early. The real profit today is made in treating diseases, not preventing them.

"Cutting Costs and Covering America: a Twenty-first Century Health Care System. University of Iowa, May 29, 2007

ON HILLARY CLINTON

She has gone through some battles that, in some cases unfairly, have created a perception about her that is different from how I am perceived.

Chicago Tribune, December 15, 2006

I think very highly of Hillary. The more I get to know her, the more I admire her. I think she's the most disciplined—one of the most disciplined people—I've ever met. She's one of the toughest. She's got an extraordinary intelligence. And she's somebody who's in this stuff for the right reasons.

New Yorker, October 30, 2006

I think that Senator Clinton is a terrific public servant. She's a smart person, she is obviously a fierce competitor. But I've said before, she was a friend of mine before this election started, and she'll be a friend afterwards. Obviously I think I'd be the better president, otherwise I wouldn't be running.

KDKA, March 31, 2008

I think Senator Clinton is smart and can be an effective advocate. But I think that the biggest difference is that Senator Clinton accepts the rules of the game as they are set up. She accepts money from PACs and lobbyists. I don't accept that politics has to be driven by those special interests and lobbyists.

60 Minutes, February 7, 2008

I have tremendous respect for Hillary Clinton. She's an outstanding leader in the Democratic Party. She's earned her stripes.

Newsweek, December 25, 2006

I think Hillary is a wonderfully intelligent and capable person. I'm sure that, should she decide to run for president, she will be a formidable candidate.

Face the Nation, March 12, 2006

ON HOMELAND SECURITY

Regarding the inspections of ports, we are currently inspecting only three percent of all incoming cargo. Terrorists could load up a cargo container and drive it straight into the middle of the Loop without significant risk of them being inspected. Our chemical and nuclear plants are still unsecured, despite how vulnerable they are. There are a whole host of domestic priorities that have been neglected by the Bush administration.

Illinois Senate Debate, October 26, 2004

ON HOW HE MAKES DECISIONS

If I look at an issue or if I look at how I approach campaigning, if it's something that is consistent with my broader values and is just a matter of tactics—having to take half a loaf—then that's something I'm comfortable with, and that's sort of the nature of the process. If it's something that violates my core beliefs, then it's not worth it.

Talk of the Nation, November 2, 2006

ON IMMIGRATION POLICY

It behooves us to remember that not every single immigrant who came into the United States through Ellis Island had proper documentation. Not every one of our grandparents or great-grandparents would have qualified for legal immigration. But they came here in search of a dream, in search of hope. Americans understand that, and they are willing to give an opportunity to those who are already here, as long as we get serious about making sure that our borders actually mean something. Today's immigrants seek to follow in the same tradition of immigration that has built this country. We do ourselves and them a disservice if we do not recognize the contributions of these individuals. And we fail to protect our Nation if we do not regain control over our immigration system immediately.

Floor Statement on Immigration Reform, April 3, 2006

We're a nation of immigrants. But if those folks are going to live in this country, they have to be put on a pathway to citizenship that involves them paying a fine, making sure that they are at the back of the line and not cutting in front of people who applied legally to come into the country. We've got to have employer sanctions that can actually be enforced. And that's probably the most important thing we can do.

Larry King Live, October 19, 2006

One of the central components of immigration reform is enforcement, and this bill contains a number of important provisions to beef up border security. But that's not enough. Real enforcement also means drying up the pool of jobs that encourages illegal immigration. And that can only happen if employers don't hire illegal workers. Unfortunately, our current employer enforcement system does little to nothing to deter illegal immigrants from finding work. We need an electronic verification system that can effectively detect the use of fraudulent documents, significantly reduce the employment of illegal workers, and give employers the confidence that their workforce is legal.

Floor Statement on the Employment Verification Amendment, May 23, 2006

ON IMPEACHING BUSH

[Someone asked me] shouldn't the president be impeached for lying? Well, with FDR, JFK, and LBJ, we have a pretty long list of presidents who maybe were not entirely forthcoming with intelligence information before they went to war, so I'd be cautious against making legal cases against the administration.

Chicago Tribune, December 5, 2005

ON THE INTERNET

We can't have a situation in which the corporate duopoly dictates the future of the Internet and that's why I'm supporting what is called Net Neutrality. And part of the reason for that is companies like Google and Yahoo might never have gotten started had they not been in a position to easily access the Internet and do so on the same terms as the big corporate companies that were interested in making money on the Internet.

"Network Neutrality" podcast, June 8, 2006

I think the danger of blogs is that we are only talking to ourselves and people who agree with us. That means that over time we are just reinforcing our own preconceptions and we are not opening up to other ideas and other points of view. One of the things I am always trying to figure out is how to get different bloggers and different points of view communicating so it is a conversation and dialogue, not just all of us cheering each other on.

Heightsmom.blogspot.com, June 4, 2006

ON IRAN

My approach to Iran will be based upon aggressive diplomacy. I will not take the military option off the table. But I also believe that under this administration, we have seen the threat grow worse, and I intend to change that course. The time has come to talk directly to the Iranians, and to lay out our clear terms: an end to their pursuit of nuclear weapons; an end to their support of terrorism; and an end to their threats against Israel and other countries in the region. To achieve this goal, I believe that we must be prepared to offer incentives, like the prospect of better relations and integration in the international community, as well as disincentives, like the prospect of increased sanctions.

Israeli daily *Yedioth Ahronoth*, February 29, 2008

Iran is a classic case of something biting us on the ankle, when we assisted in overthrowing the democratically elected regime that was replaced by the Shah.

New Yorker, January 15, 2007

78

The threat from Iran is real, and my goal as president will be to eliminate it. Ending the war in Iraq will be an important step toward
achieving this goal, because it will increase our flexibility and our
credibility when we deal with Iran. Make no mistake; Iran has been
the biggest strategic beneficiary of the war in Iraq, and I intend to
change that.

Israeli daily Yedioth Ahronoth, February 29, 2008

It's time to deliver a direct message to Tehran. America is a part of a
community of nations. America wants peace in the region. You can
give up your nuclear ambitions and support for terror and rejoin the
community of nations. Or you will face further isolation, including
much tighter sanctions.

"Remarks of Senator Barack Obama: Turning the Page in Iraq"
Clinton, Iowa, September 12, 2007

ON IRAQ

There are no good options left in this war.

"A Way Forward in Iraq" speech, November 20, 2006

We're not going to babysit a civil war.

The Today Show, January 11, 2007

I'm not opposed to all wars, I'm opposed to dumb wars. I'm opposed to rash wars. I am opposed to wars that are ideologically driven, and based on power and politics instead of reason.

Charlie Rose Show, October 19, 2006

Our troops can help suppress the violence, but they cannot solve its root causes. And all the troops in the world won't be able to force Shia, Sunni, and Kurd to sit down at a table, resolve their differences, and forge a lasting peace.

Chicago Tribune, November 21, 2006

It is time to give Iraqis their country back. I believe that it remains possible to salvage an acceptable outcome to this long and misguided war. But I have to be honest, it will not be easy.

St. Louis Post-Dispatch, November 20, 2006

We got distracted in Iraq and we ended up pursuing a course that was based on faulty intelligence, fudged numbers, and a shading of the truth, and we are seeing the results.

Larry King Live, October 19, 2006

It's not going to matter how many troops we have there. If the Iraqi people have not taken the responsibility for forming a government that recognizes the importance of all parties being involved—and, most importantly, makes certain that the government apparatus, the security apparatus, is in the hands of nonsectarians—then we are not going to be able to impose order in that country.

Face the Nation, March 12, 2006

We're still mired in a tragic and costly war that should have never been waged.

Barackobama.com

If we have a phased redeployment where we're as careful getting out as we were careless getting in, then there's not reason why we shouldn't be able to prevent the wholesale slaughter that some people have suggested might occur.

Politico.com, February 11, 2008

I don't know any military expert who says that a modest increase in troop levels is going to make a big difference. Even if you pursue the logic of increased troop levels, you're going to need one hundred thousand more, one hundred and fifty thousand more, orders of magnitude that we don't possess. Twenty thousand troops is not going to make a difference anymore.

New Yorker, January 15, 2007

The administration has narrowed an entire debate about war into two camps: "cut-and-run" or "stay the course." If you offer any criticism or even mention that we should take a second look at our strategy and change our approach, you are branded "cut-and-run." If you are ready to blindly trust the administration no matter what they do, you are willing to "stay the course."

Chicago Tribune, November 23, 2005

In the end, Iraq is not about one person's legacy, a political campaign, or rigid adherence to an ideology. What is happening in Iraq is about the security of the United States. It is about our men and women in uniform. It is about the future of the Middle East. It is about the world in which our children will live.

Speech to the Chicago Council on Foreign Relations, November 22, 2005

When we establish and send a signal through our troop withdrawals that, in fact, we are not solely responsible for putting Iraq back together again, then we start providing the space for other entities— international community, regional powers, and the Iraqis, most importantly—to join together and start thinking about what's the solution.

Charlie Rose Show, October 19, 2006

The Bush administration has been naive throughout. It was naive to think that we'd be greeted as liberators in Iraq. It's been naive in thinking that somehow this would actually diminish recruitment for terrorism. In fact, it's accelerated it. It's been naive with respect to how difficult it's been to secure the peace, and our troops and our taxpayers are suffering from those errors.

Illinois Senate Debate, October 26, 2004

It's not a great bargain for the next President to take over the mess in Iraq. But there is as much pressure in both the Republican and Democratic camps, because both have genuine concern for the troops and the families and the budget. It won't be good for congressmen of the President's party if we're still spending two billion dollars a week in Iraq in two years.

New Yorker, January 15, 2007

It makes sense for us to begin a phased withdrawal of our troops. I think it is time for us to tell the Iraqis they are responsible for their country and they've got to make a decision about how they want to live together.

Larry King Live, October 19, 2006

I'm not one of those people who cynically believes Bush went in only for the oil.

New York Magazine, October 2, 2006

We absolutely have an obligation to the Iraqi people. That's why I've resisted calls for an immediate withdrawal.

New Yorker, January 15, 2007

Every American wants to see a peaceful and stable Iraq. No American wants to leave behind a security vacuum filled with terrorism, chaos, ethnic cleansing, and genocide. But no American wants a war without end—a war where our goals and strategies drift aimlessly, regardless of the cost in lives or dollars spent, and where we end up with arbitrary, poll-driven troop reductions by the administration—the worst of all possible outcomes.

Speech to the Chicago Council on Foreign Relations, November 22, 2005

With all that our troops and their families have sacrificed, with all this war has cost us, and with no discernible end in sight, the same people who told us we would be greeted as liberators, about democracy spreading across the Middle East, about striking a decisive blow against terrorism, about an insurgency in its last throes—those same people are now trumpeting the uneven and precarious containment of brutal sectarian violence as if it validates all of their failed decisions. The bar for success is so low that it is almost buried in the sand.

"Remarks of Senator Barack Obama: Turning the Page in Iraq"
Clinton, Iowa, September 12, 2007

Let me be clear: there is no military solution in Iraq, and there never was. The best way to protect our security and to pressure Iraq's leaders to resolve their civil war is to immediately begin to remove our combat troops. Not in six months or one year—now.

"Remarks of Senator Barack Obama: Turning the Page in Iraq"
Clinton, Iowa, September 12, 2007

At every stage of this war, we have suffered because of disdain for diplomacy. We have not brought allies to the table. We have refused to talk to people we don't like. And we have failed to build a consensus in the region. As a result, Iraq is more violent, the region is less stable, and America is less secure.

"Remarks of Senator Barack Obama: Turning the Page in Iraq"
Clinton, Iowa, September 12, 2007

ON ISLAM

There are so many different interpretations of Islam as there are so many different interpretations of Christianity, that to somehow fix or define a religion based on one particular reading of the text is a mistake.

Newsweek, September 25, 2006

All of us, particularly religious leaders, have to be mindful that there are a lot of sensitivities out there. Now, the flip side is that there are those in the Muslim community who are looking to take offense and are constantly on the lookout for anything that would indicate that the West is somehow antagonistic toward Islam.

Newsweek, September 25, 2006

I do think that for the average Arab or Indonesian or Nigerian or Asian Muslim on the street that my familiarity with their culture would have an impact. I think that they would view America differently if I were president. Now, that is not just symbolic. That is something that could be used in a constructive way to open greater dialogue between the West and the Islamic world and that ultimately could make us more safe.

Beliefnet.com, January 2008

ON ISOLATIONISM

We cannot afford isolationism—not only because our work with respect to stabilizing Iraq is not complete, but because our missteps in Iraq have distracted us from the larger threat of terrorism that we face, a threat that we can only meet by working internationally, in cooperation with other countries.

Speech to the Chicago Council on Foreign Relations, November 22, 2005

We cannot afford to be a country of isolationists right now. 9/11 showed us that, try as we might to ignore the rest of the world, our enemies will no longer ignore us.

"A Way Forward in Iraq" speech, November 20, 2006

We risk a further increase in isolationist sentiment unless both the administration and Congress can restore the American people's confidence that our foreign policy is driven by facts and reason, rather than hopes and ideology.

Speech to the Chicago Council on Foreign Relations, November 22, 2005

ON ISRAEL

There are a lot of people in that area, with lots of different interests and points of view, and they all have to be taken into consideration, and we can't just rally around Sharon.

New Yorker, May 31, 2004

I will carry with me to the White House an unshakeable commitment to the security of Israel and the friendship between the United States and Israel. The U.S.-Israel relationship is rooted in shared interests, shared values, shared history, and in deep friendship among our people. It is supported by a strong bipartisan consensus that I am proud to be a part of, and I will work tirelessly as president to uphold and enhance the friendship between the two countries.

Israeli daily *Yedioth Ahronoth*, February 29, 2008

[The U.S. should] use American moral authority and credibility to help achieve Middle East peace. Our first and immutable commitment must be to the security of Israel, our only true ally in the Middle East and the only democracy. We must be consistent and we must include the EU and the Arab states in pressing for reforms within the Palestinian community.

"Renewal of American Leadership" press release, July 12, 2004

The Bush Administration's failure to be consistently involved in helping Israel achieve peace with the Palestinians has been both wrong for our friendship with Israel, as well as badly damaging to our standing in the Arab world. I do not pretend to have all the answers to this vexing problem, and untangling the issues involved is an appropriate topic for a separate speech. What I can say is this: not only must we be consistent, but we will not succeed unless we have the cooperation of the European Union and the Arab states in pressing for reforms within the Palestinian community.

Speech to the Chicago Council on Foreign Relations, July 12, 2004

ON THE ISSUES

[The] issues are never simple. One thing I'm proud of is that very rarely will you hear me simplify the issues.

MSNBC, September 25, 2006

I really have to make sure that everything I do focuses on the substance and the issues. If I stay focused on that, I'll have my good days and my bad days, but at least I'll always feel I'm on solid ground.

Chicago Tribune, February 24, 2006

A lot of the issues that I see are not an either-or situation. Rather, my perceptions about how we solve problems in health care or education span across a whole range of areas. And I want to try to capture that complexity.

Chicago Tribune, October 26, 2006

I try to describe both sides of the issue, because part of what [*The Audacity of Hope*] is about is trying to figure out how do we build common ground. Ironically, if I get criticized, usually it's because people feel that I take too much care to see all points of view.

All Things Considered, October 19, 2006

Nobody is going to be perfectly aligned with my views.

Advocate.com, April 10, 2008

ON JOBS

I would focus on improving funding for job-training programs and changing tax codes to give corporations incentives to stay in the country rather than go overseas.

Essence, March 2004

For us to tell the 55-year-old who has been working in a steel plant all his life, to suddenly retrain to become a computer scientist, that's not going to happen. What we can do is we can say, your health care is still going to be available, although you lost your job. We are going to provide you some semblance of retirement security, and we're going to protect the pension rights that you had earned.

Charlie Rose Show, October 19, 2006

We talk a lot about retraining. We don't do it very well, partly because Democrats sometimes are too suspicious of market solutions. The flip side is, sometimes conservatives have a tendency to say it will work out, folks will figure it out. And particularly in rural communities and in small towns across America, they need somebody to link them up with what are the growth jobs, what are the opportunities out there.

Charlie Rose Show, October 19, 2006

Right now, we have a tax code that gives incentives for companies to move offshore. Instead, we must have a tax code that rewards companies that are doing the right thing by investing in American workers and investing in research and development here in the United States. Our government has to be looking out for these people who are working hard everyday trying to make ends meet and right now we've got a set of policies that are not reflective of that.

"Creating Jobs in America" press release, June 21, 2004

ON JOHN McCAIN

I don't think you need a lot of imagination to figure out how they would run that campaign. "We live in dangerous times. Terrorism's looming. We need a battle-tested leader and that's John McCain." I think that's how they would present it.

Chicago Tribune, December 15, 2006

John gets excited sometimes. John's been in the Senate for close to twenty years, he's a war hero, if he wants to vent once in a while, that's not a problem. I think he has good intentions, and both of us want to see a good bill [on lobbying and ethics reform]. I did tell someone I'm going for an Emmy next [after he won a Grammy for Best Spoken Word Album]. It's going to be for Best Actor in a Drama Involving John McCain.

Time, February 13, 2006

People see John McCain as a prima donna. I think of him as a role model.

Men's Vogue, Fall 2006

ON HIS KEYNOTE SPEECH AT THE 2004
DEMOCRATIC CONVENTION

I like writing my own stuff. So I made a rare intelligent decision to start writing immediately after I was asked to deliver the speech. And so I actually had a draft completed before it was publicly announced, which was helpful, because if I'd known it was such a big deal, I might have gotten nervous and gotten writer's block.

USA Today, July 27, 2004

I am not a propagandist. That's not my job. My job and my intent in delivering a speech like this is I'm trying to speak truthfully as I can about what I see out there. If I'm restricted or prescribed in my statements because the media or Republicans—or Democrats—are going to interpret what I say through the Republican frame, I'm not going to spend a lot of time saying very much.

The Opinionator, New York Times blog, January 13, 2006

99

ON HIS LACK OF EXPERIENCE

The test of leadership in my mind is not going to be what's on a paper resume.

Chicago Tribune, December 15, 2006

I am new enough on the political scene that I serve as a blank screen on which people of vastly different political stripes project their own views. As such, I am bound to disappoint some, if not all, of them.

The Times of London, October 26, 2006

At some point people have to stop asserting that because I haven't been in the league long enough, I can't play. It's like Magic Johnson and LeBron James keep on scoring thirty [points], and their team wins, but people say they can't lead their team because they're too young.

Newsweek, January 4, 2008

I've run my Senate office, and I've run this campaign. One of the interesting things about this experience argument is that it's often posed as just a function of longevity, "I've been here longer." There are a lot of companies that have been around longer than Google, but Google's performing.

60 Minutes, February 7, 2008

I think that experience question would be answered during the course of the campaign. Either at the end of that campaign, people would say, "He looked good on paper but the guy was kind of way too green," or at the end of the campaign they say, "He's run a really strong campaign and we think he's got something to say and we think he could lead us."

Chicago Tribune, December 15, 2006

It is entirely legitimate for people to look at the body of my experience and ask the tough questions and put us through the process. If I decide to run at the end of that process, people will know me pretty well.

Milwaukee Journal Sentinel, December 11, 2006

Dick Cheney and Donald Rumsfeld have an awful lot of experience.

Vanity Fair, February 2007

ON LIBERALS VS. CONSERVATIVES

When we start breaking down into conservative and liberal, we've got a bunch of set predispositions, whether it's on gun control or health care. Any discussion about taxes ends up being are you raising them or lowering them, as opposed to the question I ask—are we raising them for high[er] income individuals that can afford it, and lowering them for lower income people who really need help? Those old categories don't work, and they're preventing us from solving problems.

Politico.com, February 11, 2008

ON HIS MARRIAGE

She [Michelle] is the smartest, toughest, funniest best friend that I could ever hope for, and she's always had my back. Whatever decision we make, we'll make together.

Washington Post, December 11, 2006

Barack didn't pledge riches, only a life that would be interesting. On that promise he delivered.

Michelle Obama in the *Sunday Times Magazine*, November 5, 2006

It is important that when I'm home to make sure that I'm present. I still forget stuff. As Michelle likes to say, "You are a good man, but you are still a man." I leave my socks around. I'll hang my pants on the door. She lets me know when I'm not acting right. After 14 years, she's trained me reasonably well.

Ebony, February 2007

She is my life partner and we make decisions together. She doesn't have a real hankering to be in the public eye or be in politics, but she has a wonderful sense of what good, solid, Midwestern, ordinary folks are thinking.

Larry King Live, October 19, 2006

She cares more about whether I'm a good father and a good husband than she does about whether I'm a U.S. senator. As she likes to say, she would be my Number 1 political supporter—she'd make calls and raise money—if I were her neighbor. She would be leading the band-wagon for me to run for President if I was married to somebody else.

New Yorker, October 30, 2006

My wife is not impressed by what's said about me in the press. She's impressed by whether I take out the garbage, take the kids to the park.

Essence, October 2006

My wife just tells me to not screw it up.

National Review, July 27, 2004

ON THE MEDIA

One of the things that I'm always battling—and I've only been on the national stage for a couple of years now—is that tendency to edit yourself so much that, at a certain point, you stop sounding like a regular person and you start taking on the persona of those bad politicians in TV movies.

Talk of the Nation, November 2, 2006

Everybody has got an ax to grind when it comes to the press. My attitude is, let the press do its job.

Hannity & Colmes, June 28, 2006

I'm surprised by the media interest in me and my candidacy. It's a little over the top, and I am not somebody who spends a lot of time reading my own press clippings.

USA Today, July 27, 2004

You're in the public eye, and people ask you the same questions over and over again, and you start giving rote answers. You become almost a caricature of yourself.

San Francisco Chronicle, October 26, 2006

I've got a wife who knocks me down a peg anytime I start believing what they're writing about me is true.

Toronto Star, October 26, 2006

ON THE MIDDLE EAST

Let's fight to make sure our so-called allies in the Middle East, the Saudis and the Egyptians, stop oppressing their own people, and suppressing dissent, and tolerating corruption and inequality, and mismanaging their economies so that their youth grow up without education, without prospects, without hope, the ready recruits of terrorist cells.

Speech at anti-Iraq War rally in Chicago, October 26, 2002

We depend on some of the most politically volatile countries in the Middle East and elsewhere to fuel our energy needs. It doesn't matter if they're budding democracies, despotic regimes with nuclear intentions, or havens for the *madrassas* that plant the seeds of terror in young minds. They get our money because we need their oil.

Crain's Chicago Business, September 4, 2006

ON THE MILITARY

Operations in Iraq and Afghanistan and the war on terrorism have reduced the pace of military transformation and have revealed our lack of preparation for defensive and stability operations. This administration has overextended our military.

Speech to the Chicago Council on Foreign Relations, July 12, 2004

We always have the right to engage militarily for our own self-defense and for our vital national interests. So I reject a false division between those who say we can only act multilaterally or we should just ignore the world. There are going to be times where we've got to act unilaterally.

Reader's Digest, September 2007

ON THE MINIMUM WAGE

I think that having the minimum wage go up every ten years is a bad idea and it's not good for small businesses, because they get socked with sudden jumps as opposed to something more gradual that they can build into their cost structures.

CNBC Closing Bell, March 27, 2008

ON MIXING POLITICS AND RELIGION

I don't think it's healthy for public figures to wear religion on their sleeve as a means to insulate themselves from criticism or dialogue with people who disagree with them.

Chicago Sun-Times, April 5, 2004

110

Those who are religious have to translate their religious-motivated agenda into universal terms that are amenable to reason. It is not sufficient if you are against gay marriage or against abortion to simply say God told me so, and then expect other people to feel, well, okay, if God is talking to you, I guess we have got to go along.

Charlie Rose Show, October 19, 2006

Today, faith drives so much of our politics, that I thought "If you don't talk about it, you are missing a whole big part of what is going on politically."

Chicago Tribune, October 26, 2004

I don't want the Democrats to suddenly pretend like they found religion if they haven't.

All Things Considered, March 10, 2005

ON THE MORTGAGE CRISIS

To prevent foreclosures, I think it is important for us to create some bottom, some floor, to give people some sense of where this ends. And so I am a strong proponent of the proposal that Chris Dodd and Barney Frank have put forward, having the FHA step in to help stabilize the market. It's not a bailout for borrowers or lenders, but what it says is we will rework some of these loan packages so that they're affordable.

CNBC Closing Bell, March 27, 2008

There are some innovative things that we can do to help people who need help, while recognizing that there are some people in the financial system who probably need to be punished for having taken some bad decisions. They were getting huge $100 million, $200 million bonuses, and they should take some hits. We don't want to bail them out. On the other hand, the ordinary person who's in their home, partly because of a deceptive loan or because their wages and incomes haven't gone up over the last seven years that George Bush was in office, those folks need some relief.

Lehrer Online NewsHour, March 17, 2008

We should put forward a $10 billion fund to help families that are in their homes that have been induced into mortgages that they can't pay, but who are willing to pay the current rates that they have. And I think that is an approach that most observers recognize will prevent the kind of moral hazards where speculators or lenders who made bad loans somehow are bailed out.

ABC News, January 26, 2008

ON HIS MULTIRACIAL HERITAGE

The starting premise for me that my mother instilled in me, and my father inadvertently instilled, was that everybody was the same.

Speech at the Aspen Institute, July 2, 2005

I've always been clear that I'm rooted in the African-American community but not limited to it.

The Washington Post, July 27, 2004

I'm certainly black enough to have trouble catching a cab in New York City.

Tavis Smiley Show, March 29, 2004

There were elements within the African-American community who might have suggested, "Well he's from Hyde Park or he went to Harvard or he was born in Hawaii so he might not be black enough." I had to make a name for myself, but having made that name, people take me at face value and don't hoist onto me a set of expectations or understandings based on something my parents did.

Chicago Tribune, June 26, 2005

The African-American community is, by definition, a hybrid culture. We draw on all these different elements. But you know, as I've grown up in the United States, I have been identified as an African-American. I'm comfortable with that identification. I'm rooted in that culture and draw inspiration from that tradition.

All Things Considered, July 27, 2004

114

I am the son of a black man from Kenya and a white woman from Kansas. I was raised with the help of a white grandfather who survived a Depression to serve in Patton's Army during World War II, and a white grandmother who worked on a bomber assembly line at Fort Leavenworth while he was overseas. I've gone to some of the best schools in America and lived in one of the world's poorest nations. I am married to a black American who carries within her the blood of slaves and slaveowners—an inheritance we pass on to our two precious daughters. I have brothers, sisters, nieces, nephews, uncles, and cousins, of every race and every hue, scattered across three continents, and for as long as I live, I will never forget that in no other country on earth is my story even possible.

"A More Perfect Union," Philadelphia, Pennsylvania, March 18, 2008

I can no more disown [Reverend Wright] than I can disown the black community. I can no more disown him than I can my white grand-mother—a woman who helped raise me, a woman who sacrificed again and again for me, a woman who loves me as much as she loves anything in this world, but a woman who once confessed her fear of black men who passed by her on the street, and who on more than one occasion has uttered racial or ethnic stereotypes that made me cringe.

"A More Perfect Union," Philadelphia, Pennsylvania, March 18, 2008

ON HIS NAME

I was told, people will remember your name and won't like it. You can have one African name, but not two. You can be Barack Smith or Joe Obama—but not Barack Obama.

Live Your Best Life, Oprah Winfrey, page 292

Some people call me Alabama.

U.S. News & World Report, August 2, 2004

ON NATIONAL SECURITY

What I think should be a national security framework that hearkens back to what we did right after World War II, and Truman and Acheson and George Marshall helped to craft a policy of containment, engagement with other countries, creating NATO, creating strong alliances, creating a set of international rules of the road that all of us could abide by.

Larry King Live, October 19, 2006

From a national-security posture, there's not a better thing we could do—for example, dealing with proliferation issues in Iran—than to drive the price of oil down to twenty-five bucks a barrel. It's the single biggest thing we could do to effectuate change and cut the legs out of some of the fundamentalist impulses in the Middle East.

New Yorker, October 30, 2006

Every democracy is tested when it is faced with a serious threat. As a nation, we have to find the right balance between privacy and security, between executive authority to face threats and uncontrolled power. What protects us, and what distinguishes us, are the procedures we put in place to protect that balance, namely judicial warrants and congressional review. These aren't arbitrary ideas. These are the concrete safeguards that make sure that surveillance hasn't gone too far.

Speech on the confirmation of Michael Hayden, May 25, 2006

ON NATIVE AMERICANS

We have to have somebody not just in the Bureau of Indian Affairs, but somebody in the White House who has my ear directly, to communicate the needs of native populations, and a commitment for me to meet at least once a year with tribal leaders and hear directly about their concerns. The Bureau of Indian Affairs has become sort of a backwater; it doesn't have a lot of clout in the administration. I want to put it front and center, because on every indicator, Native Americans are having a much tougher time than the population at large.

Great Falls Tribune, April 6, 2008

ON NORTH KOREA

Just because they're state actors doesn't mean they might not act irrationally. We can't gauge their decision-making process accurately, partly because our intelligence capabilities have been entirely inadequate to the task, and partly due to the nature of the regimes. Whatever you want to say about the Soviets, they were essentially conservative. The North Korean regime is driven more by ideology and fantasy.

New Yorker, January 15, 2007

[We should] address the threat posed by North Korea. By refusing to negotiate with North Korea for three and half years, experts believe that North Korea may now be close to having six to eight nuclear weapons. We must immediately insist on complete and verifiable elimination of North Korea's nuclear capability, engage in Six-Party bilateral talks, and facilitate a reform agenda that is broader than denuclearization to address humanitarian concerns.

"Renewal of American Leadership" press release, July 12, 2004

ON NUCLEAR WEAPONS

Let's fight to make sure that the U.N. inspectors can do their work, and that we vigorously enforce a non-proliferation treaty, and that former enemies and current allies like Russia safeguard and ultimately eliminate their stores of nuclear material, and that nations like Pakistan and India never use the terrible weapons already in their possession, and that the arms merchants in our own country stop feeding the countless wars that rage across the globe.

Speech at anti-Iraq War rally in Chicago, October 26, 2002

The issue of nuclear proliferation, an area where we can lead not only by forcing Iran and North Korea to stand down, but also by renegotiating with Russia on the ways that we can bring our own nuclear stockpiles down.

Reader's Digest, September 2007

ON HIS PERSONAL INTEGRITY

I'm very proud of how I've conducted myself during the entire time I've been in public service. My hope would be that people come away saying, "He's not perfect, but he owns up to his mistakes and tries to correct them as quickly as possible."

Washington Post, December 17, 2006

I got a free pass because I wasn't subjected to a bunch of negative ads. And nobody thought I was going to win. So I basically got into the habit of pretty much saying what I thought. And it worked for me. So I figured I might as well keep on doing it.

New York Magazine, October 2, 2006

I made some bad decisions early in my life, but as an adult I made a series of choices that I'm very proud of. I got to work on behalf of people who needed help, to advocate for the dispossessed, and took a lot of risks when a comfortable path was before me. So I think my judgments over the last twenty-five years indicate somebody who handles just about anything that is thrown at him.

Newsweek, January 4, 2008

At some level, your individual salvation depends on collective salvation. It's only when you hitch yourself up to something bigger than yourself that you're going to realize your true potential, and the world will benefit from that potential.

Diverse: Issues in Higher Education, August 10, 2006

124

When I hear "With malice toward none, with charity toward all"
being quoted, and all we have around here is malice toward all and
charity toward none, it gets me frustrated. There are risks in including
that kind of approach in a speech like that because it's a feel-good
event, but one of the things that I'm trying to be mindful of is not
starting to get so comfortable or risk-averse that I end up sounding
like everyone else.

Chicago Tribune, June 26, 2005

You should always assume that when I cast a vote or make a statement it is because it is what I believe in. The thing that bothers me is
the assumption that if I make a judgment that's different from yours,
then it must mean I am less progressive or my goals are different,
meaning I must be not really committed to helping people.

The Nation, June 26, 2006

ON HIS PERSONAL STRENGTHS

I can walk into a room, whether they're black, white, rural, urban, red state, blue state, and after thirty minutes, engage them in a conversation where they say, a lot of what this guy is saying makes sense.

Charlie Rose Show, October 19, 2006

And if you talk to my wife, she'll tell you that there are times when I do not put aside childish things; when I continually struggle to rise above the selfish or the petty or the small.

Northwestern University Commencement Address, June 16, 2006

I like to think I have a message that's useful, I like to think that I can contribute, otherwise I wouldn't have written [*The Audacity of Hope*]. There's the question of whether I am the right messenger for whatever message that is. And that's not clear as well, because, like anybody in politics, I've got strengths and I've got weaknesses, both politically and substantively.

New Yorker, October 30, 2006

I'm a self-confessed policy wonk.

Chicago Tribune, March 20, 2005

I probably always feel on some level I can persuade anybody I talk to.

Time, February 20, 2006

I feel confident that if you put me in a room with anybody—black, white, Hispanic, Republican, Democrat—give me half an hour and I will walk out with the votes of most of the folks. I don't feel constrained by race, geography, or background in terms of making a connection with people.

People Weekly, December 25, 2006

The fact that I conjugate my verbs and speak in a typical Midwestern newscaster voice, there's no doubt this helps ease communication between myself and white audiences. And there's no doubt that when I'm with a black audience, I slip into a slightly different dialect. I don't feel the need to talk in a certain way before a white audience. And I don't feel the need to speak a certain way in front of a black audience. There's a level of self-consciousness about these issues the previous generation had to negotiate that I don't feel I have to.

New York Magazine, October 2, 2006

I don't think humility is contradictory with ambition. I feel very humble about what I don't know. But I'm plain ambitious in terms of wanting to actually deliver some benefit for the people of Illinois.

Chicago Tribune, March 20, 2005

I'm comfortable in my own skin.

Rolling Stone, December 30, 2004

ON HIS POLITICAL AGENDA

I want to make real the American ideal that every child in this country has a shot at life. Right now, that's not true.

Live Your Best Life, Oprah Winfrey, page 293

Over the next six years, there will be occasions where people will be surprised by my positions. I won't be as easy to categorize as many people expect.

Chicago Tribune, March 20, 2005

My street cred as a progressive is not something I worry too much about. People can look at the ten years that I've been in politics and pull the legislation I've passed and look at my votes and get a pretty good sense of what my values are and where I'm coming from. That's not something I worry about.

Time, February 13, 2006

My job is to inspire people to take ownership of this country. Politics is not a business. It's a mission. It's about making people's lives better.

Essence, March 2004

Since the founding, the American political tradition has been reformist, not revolutionary. What that means is that for a political leader to get things done, he or she ideally should be ahead of the curve, but not too far ahead. I want to push the envelope but make sure I have enough folks with me that I'm not rendered politically impotent.

Harper's, November 2006

ON POLITICAL CAMPAIGNING

I don't know about you, but the war against terrorism isn't supposed to crop up just between September and November in even-
numbered years. That seems to be the pattern.

Salon, September 18, 2006 .

I wouldn't run if I didn't think I could win.

Chicago Tribune, December 15, 2006

We have a long and rigorous election process and, if I ever did decide
to run [for President], I'm confident that I'd be run through the paces
pretty good.

Sunday Times Magazine, November 5, 2006

The Democrats will continue to squabble. You've got at least eight Democrats running for the presidency. It means all of them have an incentive not to unify around a strategy, but to distinguish themselves, to break out of the pack. So I'd say we're gonna have some silly season going on.

New York Magazine, October 2, 2006

I'm a public figure, and I wouldn't have gone into public life if I wasn't interested in shaping the debate and moving it forward.

New Yorker, October 30, 2006

When I look at what happened in my race, the ability of the Internet to spread the word about a campaign for a candidate who wasn't that well known was absolutely critical.

Ohio State Democratic Party Dinner, June 4, 2006

ON HIS POLITICAL CAREER

I think what's worked for me has been the capacity to stay true to a set of progressive values but to be eclectic in terms of the tools to achieve those progressive values. To not be orthodox. To be willing to get good ideas from all quarters.

Washington Post, December 11, 2006

I wasn't one of these folks who at the age of five said to myself, "I'm going to be a U.S. senator." The motivation for my work has been more rooted in the need to live up to certain values that my mother instilled in me, and to figure out how you reconcile those values with a world that is broken apart by class and race and nationality. And so I guess I have on occasions had to push myself or I've been pushed into service, not always because I thought it was fun or that it was preferable to sitting down and watching a ball game, but because I felt it was necessary.

Men's Vogue, Fall 2006

My job is not to represent Washington to you, but to represent you
to Washington.

Oprah Winfrey Show, October 18, 2006

The reason I'm involved in politics right now is not because I wanted
to be JFK; it's because of the civil rights movement. And I think
about all those nameless women marching for freedom, not taking
the bus when they come home from a hard day's work doing somebody else's laundry. To me, that embodies the best of the American
spirit, and that's the standard that I measure myself by.

All Things Considered, July 27, 2004

I am under no illusion that all people throughout the state of Illinois
agree with me on every single position.

Election Night Speech, November 2, 2004

134

ON POLITICAL PARTIES

The single biggest gap in party affiliation among white Americans today is not between men and women, or those who reside in so-called red states and those who reside in blue, but between those who attend church regularly and those who don't.

Call to Renewal Keynote Address, June 28, 2006

One party seems to be defending a moribund status quo, and the other is defending an oligarchy. It's not a very attractive choice.

Newsweek, December 27, 2004

Republicans will have to recognize our collective responsibilities, even as Democrats recognize that we have to do more than just defend old programs.

Knox College Commencement Address, June 4, 2005

ON A POLITICIAN'S PAST

I'm very cautious about attributing a lot of weight to statements that were made twenty or thirty years ago. I don't think it is automatically indicative of what he thinks now.

> Regarding Judge Samuel Alito's nomination to the Supreme Court,
> *Chicago Tribune*, December 5, 2005

ON POLITICS

What you just get a sense of is that there is a political transition that is going to happen nationally, where people try to break out of some of the conservative-liberal sharp divisions.

> *Newsweek*, September 25, 2006

Our politics at its best involves us recognizing ourselves in each other. And our politics at its worst are when we see immigrants or women or blacks or gays or Mexicans as somehow separate, apart from us.

Chicago Tribune, October 26, 2006

There are times where I feel as if people are just distorting what I say to score cheap political points. And that gets you frustrated or weary or occasionally angry. And so, I try not to do that to other people.

Beliefnet.com, January 2008

If people are paying attention, then we get good government and good leadership. And when we get lazy as a democracy and civically start taking shortcuts, then it results in bad government and politics.

Newsweek, September 25, 2006

The biggest problem in politics is the fear of loss. It's a very public thing, which most people don't have to go through.

New Yorker, October 30, 2006

If you make political discourse sufficiently negative, more people will become cynical and stop paying attention. That leaves more space for special interests to pursue their agendas, and that's how we end up with drug companies making drug policy, energy companies making energy policy, and multinationals making trade policy.

New Yorker, May 31, 2004

It's not the magnitude of our problems that concerns me the most. It's the smallness of our politics. America's faced big problems before. But today, our leaders in Washington seem incapable of working together in a practical, common sense way. Politics has become so bitter and partisan, so gummed up by money and influence, that we can't tackle the big problems that demand solutions.

Barackobama.com, January 16, 2007

138

You get a sense that some of my colleagues just feel trapped by the rigidity and the lockstep nature of party politics in Washington. A couple of senators have joked about how their wrists are getting stiff because they were having to vote "no" on everything.

Chicago Tribune, March 20, 2005

What we have now is a surplus amount of conflict that is manufactured. It's manufactured in television ads, it's manufactured in terms of how the parties portray each other. There doesn't seem to be any break from the perpetual campaign. And so we never sit down and actually govern.

Charlie Rose Show, October 19, 2006

The most gratifying feeling in politics is when you hit that sweet spot where everybody concludes that the law that we've just passed works and is going to make things better, and everybody across party lines has to confess that we're probably better off with this thing than not.

New Yorker, October 30, 2006

ON HIS POPULARITY

It's always hard to stand outside yourself and know what it is that people are reacting to. Some of it is just dumb luck.

Newsweek, September 25, 2006

I would not be here had it not been for 1984, or for 1988. If I'm on the cover of *Ebony*, it's not because of me. It's because a whole bunch of folks did the work to put me there.

The Sunday Times, January 14, 2007

I have always been suspicious of our celebrity culture. And now I find myself in this odd position where I am a part of it, and to some degree a beneficiary of it. We cycle through the new and the novel, and stack story after story on top of individuals, until we lose track of who we're talking about. And if you get absorbed in that, you lose track of who you're talking about.

New Yorker, October 30, 2006

Andy Warhol said we all get our fifteen minutes of fame. I've already had an hour and a half. I'm so overexposed, I'm making Paris Hilton look like a recluse.

Sunday Times Magazine, November 5, 2006

It's flattering to get a lot of attention, although I must say it is baffling. I think to some extent I've become a shorthand or symbol or stand-in for a spirit that the last election in New Hampshire represented. It's a spirit that says we are looking for something different, we want something new.

Irish Times, December 12, 2006

There's this weird confluence of events that's making all this possible. But my experience in these kinds of things is that what comes up must come down.

Washington Post, July 27, 2004

Given all the hype surrounding my election, I hope people have gotten a sense that I am here to do work and not just chase cameras. The collateral benefit is that people really like me. I'm not some prima donna.

Chicago Tribune, March 20, 2005

I think there is a great hunger for change in the country, and not just policy change. What I also think they are looking for is change in tone and a return to some notion of the common good and some sense of cooperation, of pragmatism over ideology. I'm a stand-in for that right now.

U.S. News & World Report, January 8, 2007

I'm the flavor of the month. This is a celebrity culture, and that
culture has to be fed.

San Francisco Chronicle, October 26, 2006

I've got a celebrity that's undeserved and a little overgrown relative
to the actual power that I have in this city.

All Things Considered, March 10, 2005

ON PORK-BARREL SPENDING

Pork is in the eye of the beholder. The recipients don't tend to think
it's pork, especially if it's a great public-works project.

Harper's, November 2006

ON THE PRESIDENCY

That's the power of the presidency that I don't see used enough. The capacity to explain to the American people in very prosaic, straightforward terms: here are the choices we have. The biggest problem we have in our politics—and our campaigns press this upon candidates—is to lie about the choices that have to be made. And to obfuscate and to fudge. And so by the time the person arrives, people are already set up for disappointment.

New Yorker, October 30, 2006

I'm not sure anyone is ready to be president before they're president.

Meet the Press, October 22, 2006

America is ready to turn the page. America is ready for a new set of challenges. This is our time. A new generation is prepared to lead.

Washington Post, December 11, 2006

People who are ready are folks who go into it understanding the gravity of their work, and are able to combine vision and judgment. Having knowledge is important. I'm one of those folks—I wouldn't probably fit in with the administration—who actually thinks that being informed is a good basis for policy.

New Yorker, October 30, 2006

My attitude about something like the presidency is that you don't want to just be the president. You want to change the country. You want to make a unique contribution. You want to be a great president.

Men's Vogue, Fall 2006

One of the most important things a new president can do, is to essentially figure out what is the updated version of the post–World War II order that was structured by Truman and Acheson, and Marshall and Kennan: what does that look like? What is our national security strategy?

New Yorker, October 30, 2006

ON PRESIDENT GEORGE W. BUSH

We all remember that George Bush said in the 2000 campaign that he was against nation-building. We just didn't know he was talking about this one.

Speech to the Nebraska Democratic Party, June 14, 2006

I don't think that George Bush is a bad man. [Republicans] just believe in different things.

New York Times, September 18, 2006

I find him actually a decent person. He is an engaging person.

Charlie Rose Show, October 19, 2006

Straight answers to critical questions. That's what we don't have right now.

Washington Post, November 23, 2005

My impression is that one of the president's strengths is he's extremely sincere. And I think that he genuinely feels like he's doing the right thing. I don't think he sees hypocrisy in his actions. I think, in his mind, there's some consistency there.

All Things Considered, March 10, 2005

It is way too simplistic just to say this administration doesn't care about black people. I think it is entirely accurate to say that this administration's policies don't take into account the plight of poor people in poor communities and this is a tragic reflection of that indifference, but I also have to say that it's an indifference that is not entirely partisan.

Chicago Tribune, September 11, 2005

This has been the most ideological administration in my lifetime, even more so than the Reagan administration. The Reagan administration, despite the rhetoric, could be pragmatic.

U.S. News & World Report, January 8, 2007

Now, let me say this: I don't think that George Bush is a bad man. I think he loves his country. I don't think this administration is full of stupid people, I think there are a lot of smart folks in there. The problem isn't that their philosophy isn't working the way it's supposed to, it's that it is. It's that it's doing exactly what it's supposed to do.

Speech at Take Back America Conference, June 14, 2006

This has been probably the most ideologically driven administration in my memory. And I don't know how far I'd have to go back to find one, a combination of a House, Senate, and White House, that has been so obstinate in resisting facts, dissenting opinions, compromise. Everything is based on a set of preconceived notions that ignore whatever reality and information comes at them. I think that this administration has done great damage to this country.

New Yorker, October 30, 2006

We have an administration that believes that the government's role is to protect the powerful from the powerless.

New Yorker, May 31, 2004

We need to reclaim the American dream. And that starts with reclaiming the White House from George Bush and Dick Cheney. We're tired of tax cuts for the wealthy that shift the burden onto the backs of working people. We're tired of waiting ten years for the minimum wage to go up while CEP pay is soaring. We're tired of more Americans going without health care, of more Americans falling into poverty, of more American kids who have the brains and the drive to go to college—but can't—because they can't afford it. We're ready for the Bush administration to end, because we are sick and tired of being sick and tired.

"Remarks of Senator Barack Obama: Reclaiming the American Dream"
Bettendorf, Iowa November 7, 2007

America is the sum of our dreams. And what binds us together, what makes us one American family, is that we stand up and fight for each other's dreams, that we reaffirm that fundamental belief—I am my brother's keeper, I am my sister's keeper—through our politics, our policies, and in our daily lives.

"Remarks of Senator Barack Obama: Reclaiming the American Dream"
Bettendorf, Iowa, November 7, 2007

For too long now, this can-do spirit has been stifled by a can't-do government that seems to think it has no role in solving great national challenges or rallying a country to a cause.

"Securing Our Energy Future" speech, September 15, 2005

[The president] could take the politics out of Iraq once and for all if he would simply go on television and say to the American people, "Yes, we made mistakes." Imagine if he did that, how it would transform the politics of our country.

Chicago Tribune, November 23, 2005

I think Bush was sincere and is sincere about his desire to maintain a strong America, but there was a single-mindedness to this process that has led our country into a very difficult position. It's a consequence of that single-mindedness that we did not create the kind of international framework that would have allowed success once we decided to go in. I think that this administration is sincere but I think it's misguided.

Meet the Press, July 25, 2004

ON THE PRESIDENT HE'D BE

What I at least think about is, whether through luck or happenstance or serendipity or convergences between my biography and events, do I have a particular ability to bring the country together around a pragmatic, common-sense agenda for change that probably has a generational element to it as well?

Chicago Tribune, December 15, 2006

I'd want to be a really great president. And then I'd worry about all the other stuff. Because there are a lot of mediocre or poor presidents.

New York Magazine, October 2, 2006

I wouldn't be in this race if I didn't believe that I can lead us out of the political gridlock that has characterized us for more than just the last six years, that has characterized us for the last decade and a half.

Reader's Digest, September 2007

I will always be honest with you about the challenges we face. I will listen to you, especially when we disagree.

Presidential acceptance speech, Grant Park, Chicago, Illinois,
November 4, 2008

ON THE PRIMARY

Going up against the Clinton machine is no cakewalk. They're pretty serious about winning. They can play rough. And there's nothing wrong with that. There's no doubt that there'll be attempts on the part of the Republican Party to demonize me in a general election. But it's a lot harder to pull off. I don't start off with 47 percent of the country thinking they're not gonna vote for me.

60 Minutes, February 7, 2008

I think it would have been naïve for me to think that I could run and end up with quasi-frontrunner status in a presidential election, as potentially the first African-American president, and that issues of race wouldn't come up any more than Senator Clinton could expect that gender issues might not come up.

Lehrer Online NewsHour, March 17, 2008

One of the rules that I laid down very early in this campaign was that we will be fierce competitors but we will have some ground rules. And one of the ground rules for me is that we battle on policy differences. And that if we draw a contrast between Senator Clinton and myself, then it is based on fact, that we're not going to fabricate things. We're not going to try to distort or twist her positions.

60 Minutes, February 7, 2008

I try to measure whether what I'm saying is fair by seeing how I
would feel if I was at the receiving end of it. And, you know, there
are a number of people—there have been a number of times where
I've been criticized during the course of this campaign. And I say to
myself, Well, that's a fair criticism in the sense that I may disagree
with the criticism, but it's substantive and there's a legitimate difference of opinion.

Beliefnet.com, January 2008

ON PRIVACY

Americans fought a Revolution in part over the right to be free from unreasonable searches, to ensure that our government couldn't come knocking in the middle of the night for no reason. We need to find a way forward to make sure that we can stop terrorists while protecting the privacy, and liberty, of innocent Americans.

Speech on the confirmation of Michael Hayden, May 25, 2006

ON RACE

The world will [eventually] look more like Brazil, with its racial mix. America is getting more complex. The color line in America being black and white is out the window. That does break down barriers.

Crisis, October 1995

[Non-white candidates have] a higher threshold in establishing them-selves with voters.

Milwaukee Journal Sentinel, December 11, 2006

You don't vote for somebody because of what they look like. You vote for what they stand for.

Irish Times, November 4, 2006

The problem is not that things haven't gotten better. The problem is that they're not good enough, and we still have a lot of work to do.

Talk of the Nation, November 2, 2006

Is race still a factor in our society? Yes. I don't think anybody would deny that. Is that going to be the determining factor in a general elec-tion? No, because I'm absolutely confident what the American people are looking for is somebody who can solve their problems.

Fox News Sunday, April 27, 2008

I'm not somebody who uses race to score political points—quite the opposite. I would hope that it wouldn't just be something that I would do because I'm black, I would hope that any senator in my position would do the same thing.

Chicago Tribune, June 26, 2005

I have no doubt that there are some people who won't vote for me because I'm black. There would also be some people who won't vote for me because I'm young, because I've got big ears . . . or [because] they don't like my political philosophy.

U.S. News & World Report, February 15, 2008

[Living in Indonesia] made me realize that racism was an extension of other abuses of power. Living there you learned that people can find excuses other than race to oppress each other.

Crisis, October 1995

It was only three or four years ago where if I was standing outside of a restaurant waiting for my car, people would toss me the keys.

Charlie Rose Show, October 19, 2006

I don't want people to pretend I'm not black or that it's somehow not relevant.

Sunday Times Magazine, November 5, 2006

When you look at somebody like a Reverend Wright, who grew up in the fifties and sixties, you know, his experience of race in this country is very different than mine.

Lehrer Online NewsHour, March 17, 2008

The issue of race now has more to do with wealth and class. That isn't to say there's no discrimination or bias. But I think that if people think you can help them, whether it's in business or politics, they can look beyond color.

Essence, October 2006

Race is a continuing and enormous factor in American life. Always has been. It's sort of the fundamental stain on American life. What is also true is usually American people are more decent than a lot of folks give them credit for. Even when conflicts arise, you sometimes get the sense that they're busy, they're tired, they're stressed.

Who's Afraid of a Large Black Man? Charles Barkley, page 19

During the course of this campaign, there have been moments where people say, Well, I like Barack Obama, but not Al Sharpton. I like Colin Powell, but not Jesse [Jackson]. I like Oprah [Winfrey], but, you know, those of us who are African-American don't have that luxury. I don't have the luxury of separating myself out and being selective, in terms of what it means to be African-American in this society. It's a big, complex thing. It's not monolithic.

ABC News, March 19, 2008

We do need to remind ourselves that so many of the disparities that exist in the African-American community today can be directly traced to inequalities passed on from an earlier generation that suffered under the brutal legacy of slavery and Jim Crow.

"A More Perfect Union" Philadelphia, Pennsylvania, March 18, 2008

Most working- and middle-class white Americans don't feel that they have been particularly privileged by their race. Their experience is the immigrant experience—as far as they're concerned, no one's handed them anything, they've built it from scratch. They've worked hard all their lives, many times only to see their jobs shipped overseas or their pension dumped after a lifetime of labor. They are anxious about their futures, and feel their dreams slipping away; in an era of stagnant wages and global competition, opportunity comes to be seen as a zero sum game, in which your dreams come at my expense. So when they are told to bus their children to a school across town; when they hear that an African-American is getting an advantage in landing a good job or a spot in a good college because of an injustice they themselves never committed; when they're told that their fears about crime in urban neighborhoods are somehow prejudiced, resentment builds over time.

"A More Perfect Union" Philadelphia, Pennsylvania, March 18, 2008

ON THE RECESSION

Part of the reason we're in a recession is because we have an unbalanced economy. Look, you know, Henry Ford was the first one to say, "If I don't pay my workers enough to buy my cars, my business isn't going to be around for a long time." And when we lose that balance, what ends up happening is in the short term you've got some people who make out like bandits.

CNBC Closing Bell, March 27, 2008

ON RELIGION

When we ignore the debate about what it means to be a good Christian or Muslim or Jew; when we discuss religion only in the negative sense of where or how it should not be practiced, rather than in the positive sense of what it tells us about our obligations towards one another, others will fill the vacuum, those with the most insular views of faith, or those who cynically use religion to justify partisan ends.

Call to Renewal Keynote Address, June 28, 2006

At a time when image all too often trumps substance, when our politics all too often feeds rather than bridges division, when the prospects of a poor youth rising out of poverty seem of no consequence to the powerful and when we evoke our common God to condemn those who do not think as we do, rather than to seek God's mercy for our own lack of understanding—at such a time it is helpful to remember this man who was the real thing.

Chicago Tribune, June 26, 2005

I didn't grow up in a religious household. My mother, who was an anthropologist, would take me to church once in a while, and then she would take me to the Buddhist monastery, and then she'd take me to a mosque. Her attitude was religion was fascinating and an expression of human attempts to understand the mysteries of life.

Charlie Rose Show, October 19, 2006

I said if we were supposed to be perfect, we'd all be in trouble. So we rely on God's mercy and grace to get us through.

Chicago Tribune, March 20, 2005

I see faith as more than just a comfort to the weary or a hedge against death. It is an active, palpable agent in the world. It is a source of hope.

Chicago Tribune, June 29, 2006

I think we've got to admit the possibility that we are not always right, that our particular faith may not have all the monopoly on truth, and we've got to be able to listen to other people. You know I think one of the trends we are seeing right now, and which I think is causing so much political grief both domestically and internationally, is that absolutism has become sort of the flavor of the day.

Newsweek, September 25, 2006

ON REPUBLICANS

I think it's great that the Republican Party has discovered black people.

Irish Times, November 4, 2006

The reason they don't believe government has a role in solving national problems is because they think government is the problem.

Speech, June 14, 2006

Ronald Reagan changed the trajectory of America in a way that, you know, Richard Nixon did not, and in a way that Bill Clinton did not. He tapped into what people were already feeling, which is: we want clarity, we want optimism, we want a return to that sense of dynamism and, you know, entrepreneurship that had been missing.

ABC News, January 27, 2008

ON THE REVEREND JEREMIAH WRIGHT

Reverend Wright is somebody who, for all his good qualities, is somebody that I've had strong disagreements with for a very long time, but he's somebody who helped to introduce me to my Christian faith. He is somebody who married Michelle and I. He baptized our kids.

ABC News, March 19, 2008

He is condemning white racism, as he defines it, but he is not the white race. He is not suggesting that blacks are superior. What he's saying is that white racism is endemic in the society. Now, that's something that I disagree with. It's reflective of an anger and bitterness that is part of the black community's experience. It's a legacy of our past that isn't going away anytime soon. But in each successive generation, it hopefully lessens its grip.

ABC News, March 19, 2008

Did I know him to be an occasionally fierce critic of American domestic and foreign policy? Of course. Did I ever hear him make remarks that could be considered controversial while I sat in church? Yes. Did I strongly disagree with many of his political views? Absolutely—just as I'm sure many of you have heard remarks from your pastors, priests, or rabbis with which you strongly disagreed.

"A More Perfect Union," Philadelphia, Pennsylvania, March 18, 2008

Reverend Wright's comments were not only wrong but divisive, divisive at a time when we need unity; racially charged at a time when we need to come together to solve a set of monumental problems—two wars, a terrorist threat, a falling economy, a chronic health care crisis, and potentially devastating climate change; problems that are neither black or white or Latino or Asian, but rather problems that confront us all.

"A More Perfect Union," Philadelphia, Pennsylvania, March 18, 2008

The man I met more than twenty years ago is a man who helped introduce me to my Christian faith, a man who spoke to me about our obligations to love one another; to care for the sick and lift up the poor. He is a man who served his country as a U.S. Marine; who has studied and lectured at some of the finest universities and seminaries in the country, and who for over thirty years led a church that serves the community by doing God's work here on earth—by housing the homeless, ministering to the needy, providing day care services and scholarships and prison ministries, and reaching out to those suffering from HIV/AIDS.

"A More Perfect Union," Philadelphia, Pennsylvania, March 18, 2008

ON THE ROLE OF GOVERNMENT

My instinct is that the current generation is more interested in smart government. If the market solution works, let's go with the market solution. If a solution requires government intervention, let's do that. But let's look at what are the practical outcomes.

Meet the Press, October 22, 2006

There's a long history of believing that anything government touches is somehow Socialist. I don't understand the view. Because when I drive on the Interstate highway system—we're going to have the Highway Reauthorization this year—nobody says, "You know what? That's your highway, go fix it." I mean, we don't do a fundraiser to patch up the roads.

News conference at National Press Club, April 26, 2005

There's a component of individual responsibility in individual success, but society has a responsibility to give people the tools they need to succeed.

USA Today, July 27, 2004

They're telling us we're better off if we dismantle government. It's called the Ownership Society in Washington. But in our past there has been another term for it—Social Darwinism—every man or women for him or herself. But there's just one problem. It doesn't work. It ignores the fact that it has been government research and investment that has allowed all of us to prosper. And it has been the ability of working men and women to join together in unions that has allowed our rising tide to lift every boat.

Speech at AFSCME National Convention, August 7, 2006

Government cannot solve all our problems, but what it should do is that which we cannot do for ourselves—protect us from harm and provide every child a decent education; keep our water clean and our toys safe; invest in new schools and new roads and new science and technology.

Acceptance speech, Democratic National Convention, August 28, 2008

So many of our policy arguments are structured as either/or arguments, and I find this extraordinarily frustrating. You know, the notion that either you have got big government bureaucracies and command and control, or you're just hands off and whatever the market wants to do, let them do it.

Charlie Rose Show, October 19, 2006

They would tell me we don't expect our government to solve all our problems. We know that we have to teach all our own children initiative and self-respect and a sense of family and faith and community. But what we also know is that government can help provide us with the basic tools we need to live out the American dream.

Election Night Speech, November 2, 2004

170

ON RURAL ISSUES

Our rural communities are the backbone of Illinois. Yet, factories
have closed, jobs have disappeared, and homes and farms have been
foreclosed upon. Effective federal programs are necessary to protect
the rural economy.

ObamaForIllinois.com, May 2, 2004

ON SADDAM HUSSEIN

Now let me be clear: I suffer no illusions about Saddam Hussein. He is
a brutal man. A ruthless man. A man who butchers his own people to
secure his own power. The world, and the Iraqi people, would be better
off without him. But I also know that Saddam poses no imminent and
direct threat to the United States, or to his neighbors, and that in con-
cert with the international community he can be contained until, in the
way of all petty dictators, he falls away into the dustbin of history.

Speech at anti-Iraq War rally in Chicago, October 26, 2002

ON SECULAR SOCIETY

Secularists are wrong when they ask believers to leave their religion at the door before entering into the public square. The majority of great reformers in American history were not only motivated by faith, but repeatedly used religious language to argue for their cause. So to say that men and women should not inject their personal morality into public policy debates is a practical absurdity.

Call to Renewal Keynote Address, June 28, 2006

ON THE SENATE

When you're voting on a bill, half the time the bill is a hodgepodge—maybe more than half the time—of different things, some good and some bad. And oftentimes, particularly when you're in the minority party, you're voting on legislation that you had no input in that strikes compromises that you yourself would not want to strike.

Talk of the Nation, November 2, 2006

The budget process in particular is so undisciplined, and so opaque, that it is very difficult for any senator to know what they're voting on when it comes to budgetary matters at any given time. You've got this big monster bill. And those who control that process are able to slip in and massage and work on whatever they want.

New Yorker, October 30, 2006

There's a famous saying that every United States senator wakes up in the morning, looks in the mirror and looks at a future president. It's one of the congenital defects of serving in the United States Senate.

Larry King Live, October 19, 2006

Each time I walk onto the Senate floor, I'm reminded of the history, for good and for ill, that has been made there.

Knox College Commencement Address, June 4, 2005

Anybody who knows the U.S. Senate, knows that to be the only African American in that body is a tremendous responsibility.

Barackobama.com

The fact that I am—deservedly or not—a celebrity plays more of a role in the Senate leadership being interested in me participating in these events than the fact that I'm African-American. I receive a lot of attention. That is one form of currency in politics, and I think that people have been interested in seeing how that celebrity can help bring focus to the issues they were trying to highlight.

Chicago Tribune, June 26, 2005

The Senate is a clubby institution. Individual senators here, I have the utmost respect for and I think they do an excellent job for their constituents. But they don't really like people intruding on Senate business, and part of what we need right now is some sunshine as a disinfectant in Washington.

Speech on Lobbying and Ethics Reform, February 9, 2006

One of the toughest things about being a senator is most of the time you can't punch the box that says "none of the above."

Charlie Rose Show, October 19, 2006

The amount of publicity I have received means that I've got to be more sensitive in some ways to not step on my colleagues.

The Nation, June 26, 2006

When you think of the history of the Senate, what is striking is the degree to which this institution has single-handedly blocked the progress of African-Americans for much of our history. That's a sad testament to our institution. It's a stain on the institution. I don't perceive now that the battles that are going on in the Senate revolve around race as much as they revolve around economics.

Chicago Tribune, June 26, 2005

I'm pleasantly surprised at how much I got done. I feel like we had some concrete accomplishments. I'm surprised at the lack of deliberation in the world's greatest deliberative body. We have press releases passing in the night and floor statements nobody is listening to. And the fact that things move so slow. My last year in the Illinois Senate, I passed 26 bills in a year.

Time, February 13, 2006

Given the complexity of the issues that are involved, you can spend six years here being very busy and not get anything done.

All Things Considered, March 10, 2005

ON THE SEPARATION OF CHURCH AND STATE

Those of us who are seeking to police that line don't have to be absolutist about it. Not every mention of God in a public place oppresses folks.

Charlie Rose Show, October 19, 2006

I am concerned with maintaining the line between church and state. And I believe that, for the most part, we can facilitate the excellent work that's done by faith-based institutions when it comes to substance abuse treatment or prison ministries. I think much of this work can be done in a way that doesn't conflict with church and state.

Beliefnet.com, January 2008

ON SMALL BUSINESS

I actually want to provide more tax breaks to small businesses, because I think they are the primary generator of income.

CNBC Closing Bell, March 27, 2008

ON SPREADING DEMOCRACY

The United States should be more modest in our belief that we can impose democracy on a country through military force.

St. Louis Post-Dispatch, November 20, 2006

ON STEM CELL RESEARCH

This bill affects diseases that attack Americans regardless of their gender, age, economic status, ethnicity, race, or political affiliation. This is about a commitment to medical research under strict federal guidelines. I call on leaders in Illinois and President Bush in Washington to stop playing politics on this critical issue and expand the current policy on embryonic stem cell research so that we can begin finding the cures of tomorrow today.

Stem Cell Research Bill press release, June 16, 2004

ON TEACHING

Teaching keeps you sharp. The great thing about teaching constitutional law is that all the tough questions land in your lap: abortion, gay rights, affirmative action. And you need to be able to argue both sides. I have to be able to argue the other side as well as Scalia does. I think that's good for one's politics.

New Yorker, May 31, 2004

ON TERRORISM

We must always reserve the right to strike unilaterally at terrorists wherever they may exist.

"A Way Forward in Iraq" speech, November 20, 2006

Our battle against radical Islamist terrorism will not be altered overnight, stability in the Middle East must be part of our strategy to defeat terrorism, military power is a key part of our national security, and our strategy cannot be poll driven.

Speech to the Chicago Council on Foreign Relations, November 22, 2005

It makes more sense for us to focus on those terrorists who are active where we have evidence that in fact these countries are being used as staging grounds that would potentially cause us eminent harm, and then we go in. The U.S. has to reserve all military options in facing such an imminent threat, but we have to do it wisely.

Illinois Senate Debate, Illinois Radio Network, October 12, 2004

Let's finish the fight with Bin Laden and al-Qaeda, through effective, coordinated intelligence, and a shutting down of the financial networks that support terrorism, and a homeland security program that involves more than color-coded warnings.

Speech at anti-Iraq War rally in Chicago, October 26, 2002

The first priority of any president has to be to keep the American people safe. And so part of our power has to be deployed to deal with a very real terrorist threat. It would be naïve to think that simply through diplomacy we're going to deal with what is a set of ideologically driven fanatics. So we've got to deploy our power militarily. But what we also have to recognize is that keeping America safe involves giving other countries an investment in order. It's important to make sure that the young people in their countries are succeeding and prospering and not just looking through the glass at our own success.

Reader's Digest, September 2007

182

ON VETERANS

When you look at the Department for Veterans Affairs, I think it is unconscionable for us to stand by our troops and hoist the flag and suggest how patriotic we are at the same time as the veterans' budget is being effectively cut.

All Things Considered, March 10, 2005

One of the things that I'm going to be monitoring very closely is how are we treating the 100,000 plus veterans who are coming home, and to make sure the V.A. has the capacity to provide transition services for veterans who are leaving the service and reentering civilian life, particularly National Guardsmen and Reservists who perhaps did not expect to be fighting in a place like Iraq. It turns out that if you catch a veteran and provide them good services on the way out, they are much less likely to suffer Post-traumatic Stress Disorder and can make the adjustment.

"Honoring Our Commitment to Veterans" podcast, May 18, 2006

ON VOTER ID CARDS

Why shouldn't we require people to have a voter ID card when they vote? Don't we want to make sure voters are who they claim to be? And shouldn't we make sure non-citizens are casting ballots to change the outcome of elections? There are two problems: number one, there's no proof that there's any significant problem with voter fraud in the fifty states. There certainly is none showing that non-citizens are rushing to try to vote: this is a solution in search of a problem. Second is that historically disenfranchised groups—minorities, the poor, the elderly, and the disabled—are most affected by photo ID laws.

Floor Statement on requiring a photo ID to vote, May 24, 2006

ON WAR

The consequences of war are dire, the sacrifices immeasurable. We may have occasion in our lifetime to once again rise up in defense of our freedom, and pay the wages of war. But we ought not—we will not—travel down that hellish path blindly. Nor should we allow those who would march off and pay the ultimate sacrifice, who would prove the full measure of devotion with their blood, to make such an awful sacrifice in vain.

Speech at anti-Iraq War rally in Chicago, October 26, 2002

There is no more profound decision that we can make than the decision to send this nation's youth to war, and that we have a moral obligation not only to send them for good reasons, but to constantly examine, based on the best information and judgment available, in what manner, and for what purpose, and for how long we keep them in harm's way.

Speech to the Chicago Council on Foreign Relations, November 22, 2005

ON THE WAR ON TERROR

The war on terror has to be vigorously fought.

Illinois Senate Debate, Illinois Radio Network, October 12, 2004

Why do we make our economy hostage to some of the most hostile nations on Earth? Why would we spend $800 million a day on countries that do not have our best interest at heart and fund both sides of the war on terror?

San Francisco Chronicle, October 28, 2006

The war against international terrorism has pitted us against a new kind of enemy that wages terror in new and unconventional ways. At home, fighting that enemy won't require us to build the massive war machine that Franklin Roosevelt called for so many years ago, but it will require us to harness our own renewable forms of energy so that oil can never be used as a weapon against America.

Speech at the Governor's Ethanol Coalition, February 28, 2006

Where the stakes are the highest in the war on terror, we cannot possibly succeed without extraordinary international cooperation. Effective international police actions require the highest degree of intelligence sharing, planning, and collaborative enforcement.

Speech to the Chicago Council on Foreign Relations, July 12, 2004

Our enemies are fully aware that they can use oil as a weapon against America. And if we don't take this threat as seriously as the bombs they build or the guns they buy, we will be fighting the war on terror with one hand tied behind our back.

Speech at the Governor's Ethanol Coalition, February 28, 2006

We have utterly failed to deal with what may be one of the most significant potential terror threats to this country, and that is how we protect our chemical plants across the nation.

These plants are stationary weapons of mass destruction spread all across the country. Their security is light, their facilities are easily entered, and their contents are deadly. Unfortunately, the chemical lobby is one of the most powerful ones in Washington. They have dragged their feet, in terms of wanting to move this issue forward. I understand that there is no company out there that wants to be regulated, companies are generally allergic to any intrusion in their business decisions, but this is something of such great importance that we can't afford to rely solely on voluntary measures.

"Improving Chemical Plant Security" podcast, March 29, 2006

ON WASHINGTON, D.C.

What Washington needs is adult supervision.

Fundraising letter, October 2006

When you are in Washington, what struck me was how many really smart, capable people are around you all the time, offering you great ideas on every problem under the sun.

New Yorker, October 30, 2006

When the people running Washington are accountable only to the special interests that fund their campaigns, of course they'll spend your tax dollars with reckless abandon; of course they'll load up bills with pet projects and drive us into deficit with the hope that no one will notice.

Speech to the Chicago Council on Foreign Relations, November 22, 2005

We need to give D.C. the opportunity to elect its own representatives and have some political power on Capitol Hill. I want to deal with the homeless situation here in Washington, D.C. I think it is a travesty that we've got men—and increasingly women—families, across the street and in the shadow of this great Capitol. That shows a lack of concern, not just for the Capitol, but for America, when we allow something like that to happen. And as president of the United States I would be offended to drive by it.

Politico.com, February 11, 2008

One of the wonderful things about coming to Washington is realizing that everything you do is perceived as calculation. So I can't really spend a lot of time worrying about how my words are interpreted. All I can do is make those words as true as possible.

Morning Edition, July 14, 2006

I am not part of the Washington social set.

National Journal, March 18, 2006

ON WRITING BOOKS

Dreams from My Father was harder to write [than *The Audacity of Hope*.] At that point, I wasn't even sure that I could write a book. And writing the first book really was a process of self-discovery, since it touched on my family and my childhood in a much more intimate way. On the other hand, writing *Audacity* paralleled the work that I do every day: trying to give shape to all the issues that we face as a country, and providing my own personal stamp on them.

Amazon 20-Second Interview, October 2006

The first book was much more introspective. I was digging into sort of my past. It was more a book of self-discovery written by a young man. This book [*The Audacity of Hope*] was more a rumination on the country and where we need to go.

Knight Ridder/Tribune, October 20, 2006

I am somebody who usually writes out the rough draft in longhand. Then I type it into the computer, and that is where I do my editing. I find that if I write it on the computer, I go too quick. So I like getting that first draft out and then typing it in; you are less self-conscious about it.

Chicago Tribune, October 26, 2006

I guess you'd have to say I wasn't a politician when I wrote *Dreams of my Father*. I wanted to show how and why some kids, maybe especially young black men, flirt with danger and self-destruction.

The New Yorker, May 31, 2004

When I sat down to write [*The Audacity of Hope*], my intention was not to write a political manifesto, a 10-point plan for where the country needs to go. The very specific objective of this book was to say there are a set of common values and common ideals that we hold as Americans that need to be excavated, that we need to affirm, that Republicans, Democrats, independents can all buy into.

Charlie Rose Show, October 19, 2006

Even though I hadn't written a book before, I had a sense of what it felt like to write something that rang true. When you start writing you are able to discern where you're being false, where you're using clichés, where you're manufacturing emotion that's not really there, or where you're shying away from something that isn't necessarily flattering.

Men's Vogue, Fall 2006

The Audacity of Hope is not a campaign book. It's me trying to describe the moment I see us being in. Like in my chapter on foreign policy—yeah, I talk about Iraq, but I'm not laying out the ten steps we need to get out of Iraq. I spend more time talking about how, historically, we got to this place.

New York Magazine, October 2, 2006

When I write, I try to be as honest as I could. That's harder when you're in political life, because I think there's a strong impulse to try to control your image as much as possible. I found that the best way for me to approach quote, unquote, "image making" is to be myself and let there everybody know what I'm thinking. And that way, I don't end up tripping myself up saying one thing and doing another.

All Things Considered, October 19, 2006

I would feel very uncomfortable putting my name to something that was written by somebody else or co-written or dictated. If my name is on it, it belongs to me.

Chicago Tribune, March 31, 2006

CPSIA information can be obtained at www.ICGtesting.com
Printed in the USA
BVOW06s1122140716

455560BV00014B/100/P